# Northern Sinfonia:
# a magic of its own

(The title derives from 'The Sinfonia has a magic of its own'
*Middlesbrough Evening Gazette* December 1959)

Bill Griffiths

Published by Northumbria University Press, Trinity Building, Newcastle upon Tyne NE1 8ST, UK

First Published 2004

Copyright © Bill Griffiths

All rights reserved. No part of this publication may be reproduced or transmitted in any form or by any means, electronic or mechanical, including photocopy, recording, or any information storage and retrieval system, without permission in writing from the publisher. This book is sold subject to the condition that it shall not, by way of trade or otherwise, be lent, re-sold, hired out or otherwise circulated without the publishers prior consent.

British Library Cataloguing in Publication Data. A Catalogue Record for this book is available from the British Library.

**ISBN 1-904794-07-6**

## Acknowledgements

This guide to Northern Sinfonia's activities over the last five decades draws freely on archive material deposited by the Orchestra's management with the Centre for Northern Studies, Northumbria University, in 2002.

Thanks to The Sage Gateshead, the Centre for Northern Studies and Northumbria University Press for their assistance and support in this work. I am particularly grateful to Lucy Bird and Tony Froud for their comments on the draft text. Their guidance has been essential in making sense of this complex story. Thanks also to members of the Orchestra and staff, past and present and members of Friends of Northern Sinfonia, who have contributed to the research. Any infelicities remaining I take this opportunity to accept responsibility (and apologise) for.

Words can never hope to be as beautiful as musical sounds, but constitute a practical medium in which to celebrate a remarkable musical enterprise.

Bill Griffiths
*November 2004*

# Contents

Chapter One      1
    *Starting out*

Chapter Two      13
    *The orchestra*

Chapter Three      37
    *The concert*

Chapter Four      75
    *Logistics, outreach, education and advance*

Appendices      101
    *Officers of the Orchestra*
    *Artistic Directors/Conductors*
    *General Managers*
    *Members of Northern Sinfonia*

Bibliography and Sources      104

Michael Hall, founder of the Orchestra

# Chapter One
## *Starting out*

*'The provision of good music, well played, is our function.'*

Northern Sinfonia programme note, Whitley Bay, September 1962

### At the start: 1958

Music is a part of North East life. However, in the late 1950s, music and quality of life alike left a lot to be desired, and an orchestral concert was something that had to be supplied from outside. As Anthony Adams reported in *The Guardian* (14 Dec 1959):

> 'The three-quarters of a million people of Tyneside are unfortunately placed in relation to the orchestral centres of the country. A hundred and forty miles from the Scottish National in Glasgow, 130 from the Hallé in Manchester, and a few miles farther from Liverpool – they are visited by these orchestras, but infrequently. The Lemare Orchestra comes three or four times, perhaps, in a year, but it could not be said that Newcastle offered any really planned musical fare to its audiences...'

Not quite a musical limbo, but discouraging enough to rouse the constructive anger of one young north-easterner who returned home in 1956 after studying music in London – Michael Hall. His determination to put Newcastle on the musical map – and do a service to the region and the wider musical community – has become deservedly celebrated.

As Michael recalled some 25 years later:

> 'I went to Jarrow one day across on the ferry from North Shields and decided something had to be done about music in Newcastle. There was no orchestra locally and no likelihood of one starting. I made the decision to start one while I was on the ferry. In those days before they started building it up, Jarrow was like a wilderness, derelict and I thought that was typical of music in the North East.' (*The Journal*, 16 Sep 1983)

The desolate Jarrow of post-war privation became a vivid and affecting image of the need for cultural renewal – and if he could, Michael would take action, through the best means open to him – the medium of music! Not as some nostalgic return to past values, but in the sense of classical music as a living developing tradition that could be made available to everyone: a music that represented the best the world of the arts could offer.

The impetus was there in 1958; and so too, was the opportunity. Discouraged by the financial risks and the logistics of travel, it seemed doubtful whether the Hallé or the Royal Liverpool Philharmonic would be able to visit Newcastle in the 1958–59 season, leaving the door wide open for a local orchestra to offer its services.

Fortunately, Michael Hall had sufficient flair for organising, enough contacts in the musical world, and more than enough motivation to set about establishing a new orchestra on Tyneside. For two years he had been working with an amateur group, the Tyneside Chamber Orchestra, and though that was a very different matter from mounting a concert season on a professional basis, it had given him the confidence and experience to move ahead when – against all probability – the opportunity arose.

On 6 July 1958, Michael Hall wrote to Newcastle's Special Committee for the Encouragement of Cultural Activities:

> 'It has long been felt for some time by music lovers and musicians in the City and District that a first-class orchestra should be formed to give regular performances in the City Hall with a wide musical interest. The number of Symphony Concerts which music lovers have been able to attend have become diminished over the last years and this is a serious attempt to redress the balance. As considerable financial risk is involved I would like the Cultural Committee to consider if it could give a grant of financial assistance or alternatively a grant against financial loss...' (Archive 7/12)

Councillor Gladys Robson, elected Chair of the Cultural Committee in June, took note of this campaign to provide the North East with its own orchestra, and of the complementary (if not quite rival) request for funds for Eric Caller's concert series, using visiting orchestras. Diplomatically, she supported a move to re-think the whole approach to arts subsidy in the region. Consideration was given to how the arts could be best supported in the long-term – a debate that led to the formation of the North East Association for the Arts (NEAA), a co-operation between local councils to pool funding for an arts budget. It was, as Michael Hall later put it, 'the beginning of the local authorities working together not only for the Sinfonia, but for music and for industry.' (BBC film *Workshop* 1966)

In the interim, though a small grant was available from the civic authorities, the main outlay for that first season had to be met from the savings held by Michael Hall's parents, an act of faith in the future of the region and the orchestra, that was to prove richly justified.

## The first season

A major chore for Michael Hall proved to be assembling a body of skilled players. From *The Guardian* (14 Dec 1959):

> '... His problems were enormous. There were few local players of adequate standard, and that meant he had to bring them from elsewhere. After scouring the North for remnants of the Yorkshire Symphony Orchestra, tapping the Manchester and Liverpool freelance pool, and finding a few from Scotland, he still had to bring most of them from London, and that meant that for an ordinary string player the travelling expenses were nearly double his actual fee...'

Arranging the most cost-effective use of the musicians became an essential factor in that first season. Concerts were deliberately scheduled for a Wednesday to take advantage of the cheap midweek rail tickets available from London. The players would be billeted on friends overnight, and returned south on Thursday!

As Michael's sister, Jennifer, recalled:

> 'My father spent a long time doing the publicity and many other practical things. My mother entertained the musicians in our house who came for the first concerts. They were basically friends and colleagues from the Royal College of Music where Michael had studied. That first period was fun and very exciting. There was always a bit of nervous anticipation before any concert...' (*40 Years*)

By August 1958, Michael had secured, 'about 16–17 strings from London for the first concert and 18–19 for (the) remaining five,' though he later had to send out an 'S.O.S. for violinists for 24 September!' (Archive 7/1). The sum of efforts proved successful, and with 37–40 players lined up, the first season (1958–1959) of the 'Sinfonia Orchestra' got underway, with six concerts in the City Hall, Newcastle, spaced approximately a month apart.

*Northern Sinfonia and The Sinfonia Chorus at City Hall, Newcastle*

## Would it work?

'The Sinfonia Orchestra made its debut last night in the City Hall, Newcastle, and astonished the audience by the high-quality of its playing. The new orchestra, of about 40 players, led by Jürgen Hess is composed largely of imported players from London, but contains some of the best local players.' (Tom Little in *The Northern Echo* 25 Sep 1958)

The performances were impressive enough to draw the attention of the BBC and with extra funding from local cellist Valentine Orde, a concert was arranged for 21 May 1959 at the end of the first season to be broadcast on radio's prestigious *Third Programme*. It included a concerto by Charles Avison, the Newcastle-born eighteenth century composer.

National admiration of this new project was soon to follow: the *Evening Chronicle* of 18 September 1959 recorded messages of support for Northern Sinfonia from Sir Adrian Boult, Leon Goossens, Dame Myra Hess and Sir Malcolm Sargent, who wrote:

'So far as the public is concerned, of course, nothing could exaggerate the importance of maintaining the cultural life of the North by supporting this symphony orchestra.'

## Moving on

For the first three seasons, the Sinfonia remained a freelance band performing with a regular nucleus of players, but it had been Michael Hall's intention from the start to found a permanent chamber orchestra for the region, which required much more than family funds.

A good deal of support for the second and third seasons was provided by Tyne Tees Television, like the Sinfonia, a new venture in the North East. Michael Hall approached Programming Director, Bill Lyon-Shaw and was offered one show a month for the Orchestra's 1959–60 season.

The success of this and subsequent series enabled Michael Hall to bring in high-quality players and expand the Sinfonia's activities in those seasons – concerts would now be given in Middlesbrough, Carlisle, Darlington, Sunderland and Scarborough as well as Newcastle itself. However, in order to reduce costs, the concerts were concentrated into a week or less each month.

The scope of Northern Sinfonia was expanding rapidly, but it was left to Michael Hall to shoulder most of the organising work, on top of lecture courses and other work. The *Evening Chronicle* summarised it as follows:

*Michael Hall conducting*

'Michael Hall was then all things – general manager, secretary, artistic director, conductor, and fund-raiser. Perhaps his hardest job was making the rounds of the local authorities, trying to persuade them to give money to keep the Orchestra going.' (12 Oct 1973)

To assist Michael Hall, Deidre Millar was appointed Orchestral Manager: an ideal choice, she, 'had been at the Royal College at the same time as Michael Hall and had in the mean-time worked for the Arts Council and was a practising musician herself, with a good deal of organising know-how.' (Barrie Hall in *Music Teacher*, Oct 1959) Dubbed the youngest orchestral manager in the country, further promotion was not long in coming, as she and Michael married in 1960.

## Formal status

While machinery was being put in place that would encourage local councils to fund the arts in the North East, a parallel effort at constitutional evolution was taking place within the Sinfonia itself. To be eligible for central Arts Council funding the Sinfonia needed to incorporate itself as a formal association. Having proved its worth during the season of 1958–59, the Orchestra was ready to take this next step: a meeting was advertised for 23 March 1959 (see right).

As the *Evening Chronicle* reported the next day (with excusable hubris):

'NEWCASTLE gets its own ORCHESTRA

... More than 100 music lovers went to the Durant Hall, Newcastle, last night, to form the Sinfonia Concert Society, which will guarantee support for the Orchestra's activities...'

*Sir Humphrey Noble, first Chairman*

In this move to incorporation, Michael Hall had initially sought the support of Louis Towb and Charles Hereward Brackenbury, local music enthusiasts. However, it was Brackenbury's distinguished cousin, Sir Humphrey Noble, who became the first Chairman proper and made a notable contribution to putting the Sinfonia on a permanent footing.

Sir Humphrey came from a family well-versed in higher finance and with strong links with Armstrong Whitworth; he himself had a distinguished career in accountancy. His influence enabled him to obtain an overdraft for the Sinfonia of up to £4,000 at Martin's Bank, on his personal guarantee – without that facility, the day-to-day running of the Orchestra would have been nigh-on impossible – he also had a strong and genuine interest in classical music, including acting as patron of the Hexham Music Festival.

In the assessment of Tom Little, music critic of *The Northern Echo*:

'As Chairman of the Orchestra's Management Committee Sir Humphrey had some obvious advantages. He brought a bit of upper-class prestige to the enterprise; he had many excellent contacts; and he was, of course, well-heeled. He was a martinet in management but he was unique in that along with his acumen went his musicality ...' (*Prospectus 1983–84* p. 40)

---

**SINFONIA CONCERTS SOCIETY**

If you are interested in assisting the Sinfonia Orchestra in a practical way you are invited to attend a meeting at the DURANT HALL, Oxford Street, Newcastle, on Monday, March 23rd, at 7-30 p.m. The purpose of this meeting is to form a Concert Society to be responsible for the future activities of the Orchestra. Mr. Charles Brackenbury will be in the chair, and Michael Hall will give a report of this Season's concerts and proposals for future activities.

Under the chairmanship of Sir Humphrey, one important step in stabilising the basis of the Orchestra itself was taken – from September 1961, a core of 19 permanent players would be engaged.

In Sir Humphrey's words:

> 'It is perfectly true the Northern Sinfonia Concert Society was founded in 1958... but the Orchestra then was only an "ad hoc" body, all that we could afford at that time, engaged for a number of concerts five or six times in the season. They came together, rehearsed, played the concert and then dispersed. There was no chance that such an orchestra could ever get much better under such circumstances.
>
> In 1961, the really important decision was taken to form a small permanent resident professional orchestra of the highest standard. This orchestra, by playing constantly together, has already achieved a high standard as an ensemble; this is the orchestra which was specially chosen to go to [the festival at] Menton... The Northern Symphony Orchestra is now in a much higher class.'
> (*Northern Despatch* 26 Sep 1963)

Operating in this 'higher class' presented its own problems. Access to grants was opened up (and there were encouraging donations from the Calouste Gulbenkian Foundation, the Musicians' Union and Tyne Tees Television) – but expenditure was also rising, and these new sources of income could not disguise the poor financial condition of the Sinfonia – 'great difficulties' was how Sir Humphrey termed it in *The Northern Echo* of 22 June 1962. His generous solution was to make £10,000 – a really considerable sum in those days – available to the NEAA to boost the operations of that body, on the understanding that it would be used to assist the Sinfonia – and in the hope of prompting further similar contributions from industry. (Some sponsorships did indeed follow – from H.O. & W.D. Wills and the 'Big Four' banks.)

However, the increasingly dominant role of Sir Humphrey was arguably a factor in unsettling Michael Hall. Hard-pressed by the increasing demands made on him as conductor, and keen for study leave, he ended up tendering his resignation. Despite moves by Valentine Orde to renew Michael Hall's contract, the situation was set to change. Already in the 1963–64 season, substitute conductors would have to be brought in. From the autumn of 1964, other arrangements would have to be made.

## To municipalise or not?

The possibility that Northern Sinfonia might be taken on – and primarily financed – by Newcastle City Council became an issue in 1965.

> 'A move to transform the Northern Symphony Orchestra, the only permanent chamber music orchestra in the country, into a municipal orchestra, under Newcastle Corporation, was made yesterday, when members of the Orchestra's Executive Committee met the city's Cultural Activities Committee...' with a view to the Corporation taking over 'full responsibility' for the Orchestra. (*The Northern Echo* 20 Nov 1965)

'What the Orchestra was looking for was "a parent" more than anything,' explained *The Northern Echo*. This 'adoption' (as it was soon tagged in the Press) was supported by Tom Bergman (Public Relations Officer) and Sir Humphrey on the Orchestra's side and that 'arch-planner of the region' Dan Smith, on behalf of the City. Sir Humphrey doubtless wished to see the Sinfonia's future safe before he retired as chairman; Dan Smith had regard to the City of Newcastle's need to raise its profile in this country and abroad, and attract much needed new industry into the region.

However, neither the Orchestra itself nor the majority of its Management Committee favoured the move, and Newcastle's own Cultural Affairs Sub-committee seems to have been equally luke-warm. The move to municipalise died away as mysteriously as it had begun. Northern Sinfonia held true to its original conception as a chamber orchestra, and rejected the temptation to expand into a full-scale city-style symphony orchestra, to the Orchestra's ultimate gain or loss. As conductor Boris Brott bluntly put it, 'We stuck our necks out by keeping it at its present size instead of making it a large, inferior provincial orchestra.' (*The Journal* Nov 1982)

The solution to the need for long-term funding came from a different quarter. Northern Arts and the Arts Council of Great Britain, combined, undertook to clear the Orchestra's deficit in return for reform of the Management Committee, on which the two arts councils and members of the Orchestra would now have a voice. This solution was accepted at the Annual General Meeting (AGM) of September 1967– despite a desperate message from Sir Humphrey, then ill in hospital. After this momentous decision for reform, Sir Humphrey was honourably re-elected Chairman, but his illness led to his reconsidering this role by the end of the year. Sadly, this major figure in the Sinfonia's development passed away in August 1968, though something of the family tradition was sustained in his more tractable cousin Charles Brackenbury taking over as Chairman for a while. Despite this outward show of continuity, a significant shift had undoubtedly occurred and no longer was Northern Sinfonia to rely on the steering hand of a powerful if benevolent Chairman. The formula for the future was to be financial acumen, efficiency in management, and the merit of the Orchestra itself.

### 'WE ARE LOOKING FOR SOMEONE WITH DRIVE, INITIATIVE AND ABILITY...'

announced the Sinfonia (Archive 5/1/19), as it entered a new phase. The answer turned out to be the appointment of Keith Statham as General Manager on 1 August 1966.

His determination and expertise were clearly exactly what was needed, and his reforms matched the progress the Orchestra was making musically under the new direction of Rudolf Schwarz.

Statham's strategy was two-fold: very careful budgetary management (including accurate forecasting) and maximising all potential sources of income.

A firm approach to the vagaries of accounting was essential to reassure grant bodies, who were keen to see Northern Sinfonia on a sustainable financial footing.

The recommendations and aspirations of Newcastle councillors to see the Orchestra play a wider public role were by no means lost sight of.

'When our General Manager Keith Statham was appointed, he became convinced that the Orchestra's

*Keith Statham, General Manager 1966–1974*

field of activity, and hence its reputation, was too restricted for it ever to earn the money that it would need for survival. As a matter of deliberate policy, therefore the Orchestra played further afield in this country and, of course, abroad as well. That we were right to allow Stratham to pursue this policy we can see from the fact that engagements now offered to the Orchestra extend from the south coast to Scotland, from the Bath festival to the Aldeburgh festival.' (AGM 1967)

By September 1968, the advance engagements for 1969–70 had been successfully arranged, leading Chairman Charles Brackenbury to comment:

> '... this list was extremely impressive, especially when one remembered that only a few years ago the Orchestra would at this stage in the year still have been searching for work for the latter part of the same financial year. He [Brackenbury] wished expressly to remind the Management Committee of the significant increase in the number and importance of paid engagements and in the number of promotions with major international soloists and conductors since Mr. Statham and Mr Froud had been on the administrative staff.' (AGM 1968)

London concerts, though likely to involve financial loss, were seen as, 'essential to the Orchestra for reasons of internal satisfaction and prestige both within the profession and *vis-à-vis* the concert-going public in general.' (Finance Mins 19 Jan 1972)

Through George Malcolm, Statham secured a number of successful tours of Germany, assisted by The British Council and with excellent benefits in income and publicity achieved the engagement of the Orchestra for Glyndebourne Opera's summer tours (so successfully that for the summer of 1970 the Sinfonia were asked to undertake two tours).

In the field of education, while recognising that, 'for the sake of future audiences, it was of prime importance to interest the children in schools,' Statham recommended that schools be more realistically charged for educational concerts since, 'we were in fact subsidising Education Authorities.' (Man. Mins 22 Jan 1968). In March 1968, he approached Sir Robert Mayer with a view to running a series of Saturday morning concerts for children, in Newcastle. These were in place by the autumn of 1968 and proved a great attraction.

Beyond this, a considerable amount of Statham's initiatives were aimed at long-term benefits. It was through Statham that recordings for the Sinfonia were set up with EMI in 1970 and he strongly advocated the need for the Sinfonia to have its own choir. Perhaps the most impressive new initiative during this time was the plan for a brand-new rehearsal hall at 41 Jesmond Vale. This was to provide space for the Orchestra (and its amateur chorus) to rehearse and make recordings as well as supplying permanent administrative office space.

The efforts of staff and players paid off. In February 1968, Statham noted that the Sinfonia 'earned at least half of its own keep.' (Finance Mins 7 Feb 1969). If grants and other sponsorships were essential to the Orchestra's survival, it could nonetheless be claimed with some justice in 1970 that, 'the Sinfonia had raised itself by its own efforts.' (Finance Mins 1 Sep 1970).

By November 1971:

> '... the Chairman was pleased to see how expenditure had been kept under control and considered that the actual and budgeted surpluses were very satisfactory and called for congratulations to the General Manager on his administration.' (Finance Mins 11 Nov 1971)

The Northern Sinfonia had survived its tenth year and was definitely on the way up!

## Entering the inflation zone

The 1970s were to bring their own challenges. Principal conductor Rudolf Schwarz, in his mid-60s, indicated his wish to wind down his heavy responsibilities with the Orchestra. Statham retired in the spring of 1974 after eight years with the Sinfonia (he later served as successful manager of the Hong Kong Festival). Yet because of these two, standards of musical achievement and administrative competence were established that were to help sustain the Orchestra through the difficulties caused by inflation, local government reorganisation and the rethinking of Arts subsidy strategies over coming years.

The 1970s saw massive inflation, peaking at 24% in 1975, and not falling significantly until the mid-1980s. This new economic factor was in effect reducing the Sinfonia's income from grants, for although some grant increase was forthcoming, as early as 1974 it was noted that 'present inflation was already surpassing the amount of grant increase for the present year.'
(Finance Mins 28 Aug 1974)

Much appreciated assistance came from the BBC when James Langley at their Manchester studios arranged 76 broadcasts for the Sinfonia in one year (each broadcast involving two sessions of work – rehearsal and performance). Many other former and new friends of the Sinfonia rallied round to help: members of the Orchestra held fund-raising coffee mornings and soirées in collaboration with the Friends of the Sinfonia and the Ladies Committee organised some very successful Viennese Balls.

The easing of inflationary pressure coincided, fortuitously, with the Sinfonia's Silver Jubilee, and the season of 1983–84 was marked with a gala concert at the Royal Festival Hall. This was made possible by a special London Silver Jubilee Trust Committee 'made up largely of émigré Sinfonia supporters,' (AGM 1983) who raised funds and assisted in organising the event.

A special birthday concert on Saturday 24 September 1983 at Newcastle City Hall featured John Lill playing Mozart's Piano Concerto in D minor K466, and Richard Hickox conducting Beethoven's 'Eroica' (signalling the intention to record the whole cycle of Beethoven symphonies over the coming years). Other highlights of the season were Tamás Vásáry playing and directing the Janácek Concertino, Ida Haendel playing the Beethoven Violin Concerto, Sir Charles Groves conducting Haydn's Symphony no.101, and a performance of the tremendous Bach St Matthew Passion at Easter 1984. Nor was that all. The end of the 1983–84 season was marked with a tour of the western USA in October!

*Northern Sinfonia Yearbooks*

The emphasis throughout was properly on music, but we should not forget a significant 25th year commemorative publication, compiled by Tony Froud, which brought together contributions from founder Michael Hall, music critic Tom Little, James Langley of the BBC, and many others. It remains the most significant and useful account of Northern Sinfonia's progress up to 1983, as well as a splendid celebration in text and photo of that very special season.

## The new look

Fundraising and the work of The Northern Sinfonia Trust on a Development Fund had worked well to sustain the Orchestra's activities, but a new challenge arose as Arts policy shifted away from overdependence on public subsidy. In the 1980s, the Orchestra was necessarily alert to the urgent need for commercial sponsorship – the forging of reciprocal relationships in which companies could hope to gain by, 'the association of their product with excellence.' (AGM 1983)

The dissolution of the Tyne & Wear 'super-authority' in1986 and its implications for the grant mechanism underlined the need of Northern Sinfonia to mobilise alternative sources of income. By 1987, commercial sponsorship was bringing in about £75,000 a year and a welcome boost to fund-raising came in 1985 with the willingness of Catherine Cookson to lend her name to the Development Appeal.

John Myerscough's influential report, 'The Economic Importance of the Arts in Britain' (1988) had shown that the arts and culture business was a major industry in its own right (as part of the 'non-profit or value-led sector') and the corollary to this was that many a charitable and cultural organisation was enabled, and in a sense, obliged, to start thinking of its operation in more strictly self-sufficient business terms.

With emphasis on self-help and financial viability rather than social provision and grant-aid, Northern Sinfonia had to work harder than ever to maximise sources of alternative income. As reported at the 1989 AGM:

> 'Current government policy is to encourage arts organisations to reduce their reliance upon public subsidy and to increase self-generated income. For the second year running earned income has outstripped public funding through a further upturn in box office and engagement income, and through the continuing and expanding commitment of our business sponsors...'

Commercial sponsorship – advocated long since by Sir Humphrey Noble – was indeed to prove an important route forward, but an overhaul of Northern Sinfonia's administration could not be put off.

The nomination of Tony Pender to the Management Committee in 1987 (later to become Chairman) is reckoned significant in mobilising opinion for this new push forward. Under his guidance a Corporate Plan was prepared – 'a kind of mission statement of what is going to be done and how, with the intention of helping the administration to produce a detailed operational plan.' In general terms,

> '... the purpose was to run the Society in accordance with modern business practice so that it could continue to advance as an arts organisation in the current economic climate.' (AGM 1988)

Action was especially needed on improved planning and budgetary control. An EGM was called for 6 December 1988, at The Sinfonia Centre, Jesmond Vale, at which the articles of association of the Sinfonia were modified, making the Management Committee the Board of Directors. At the 1989 AGM:

> 'Bob Tilley introduced the finance report by identifying the need for a positive approach to be

taken in a carefully controlled financial policy supporting artistic excellence. He said that high income and sponsorship targets had been achieved against a background of erosion of grant value but that expenditure had disappointingly got out of control. Solutions needed to be found within the organisation and the need to increase self-generated income was paramount.'

The changes in organisation and approach were in place by 1990: John Summers became Chief Executive, and new posts of Head of Finance, and Education and Outreach Officer were created. The company was to be organised on three sectors: finance, marketing ('to match the benefits offered to needs of customers') and production (i.e. the concerts themselves).

The Chief Executive pointed out that, 'for the Society to cease its activities was not an option, and so it was necessary to carry on working against this background' (AGM 1990) – a timely reminder that the point behind this programme of change was the survival and development of the Orchestra itself in a changing economic climate. In 1985–86 grants had formed 63% of Northern Sinfonia's income; by 1990–91 that figure was reduced to 48%, illustrating the importance, indeed the necessity, of self-generated income (ticket sales, commercial sponsorship, charitable donations, the hiring of Northern Sinfonia by other concert promoters, radio and TV work). Nonetheless by 1993 there was an accumulated deficit of £117,514, only coped with by a generous 10-year interest-free loan of £100,000 from Newcastle City Council. It was never going to be easy.

John Summers was keen on the advantages of the new technology and oversaw the introduction of the computerised box office system as well as making a major contribution to broad planning. 'John was dedicated to getting what was then known as the Regional Music Centre off the ground to which end he worked tirelessly and was also involved in launching Young Sinfonia.'

(Archive 7/8). The emphasis was to be on, 'quality itself, classicism, excellence, an element of youth and a touch of excitement.' (*Inside Story*)

With regard to expert planning, Northern Sinfonia produced its Corporate Plan 1988–1991 and Development Plan 1991–1994. Complementary to these, the Arts Council undertook its own appraisal of the Orchestra in 1994 which provides a useful summary of Northern Sinfonia's situation in the early 1990s. Such studies generated a considerable amount of useful analysis and guidance for Northern Sinfonia – but in retrospect there emerges from it one major plank in the Orchestra's bridge to the future: the scheme for a new concert hall complex ('Sinfonia-plus-Music-Centre') to serve Tyneside and the region as a centre for its combined musical activities: a startling concept in its way, that would place Northern Sinfonia at the heart of an ambitious rationalisation of the region's musical needs, as a hub of music-making activity for the whole of the northern region.

> 'A feasibility study has recently [1992] been undertaken by John Myerscough which explores the economic and artistic viability for such a proposal. The new concert hall will provide a new home base for the Northern Sinfonia with a capacity more appropriate for a chamber orchestra yet also highly suitable for symphonic provision. The plans also include the concept of a regional music centre which would serve Northern Sinfonia as a core resource and provide a radical new national model. It is intended that the Orchestra will employ an additional 18 players/teachers who will teach in the centre...' (Arts Council Report, Archive 3/2/25)

It was indeed an attractive proposition, but one that had to be carefully thought through and planned, and would take over a decade to reach fruition.

*Northern Sinfonia, leader Bradley Creswick*

# Chapter Two
## *The orchestra*

*'Music is everywhere. One way or another we all make music. We speak, sing, whistle and hum. We are all musicians.'*

Joan Elliott in *The Viewer* no. 455 (1967)

## What's in a name?

The Orchestra of 1958 depended on freelance players and did not as such have a permanent composition, but it did have a purpose, and some care was taken in selecting a title that would convey the appropriate sense of potential combined with economy of forces. Michael Hall explained the process as follows:

> 'In consultation with a viola pupil who was a sub-editor on *The Journal* I selected the title "Sinfonia" because it best suggested my intentions: an orchestra which would be small enough to play in modestly-sized halls, yet large enough to play the bulk of the Baroque and Classical repertoire and a fair proportion of the Modern, as well.' (*40 Years*)

(The prefix 'Northern' was added in 1959; the extra tag 'of England' was sometimes added when playing abroad.)

What size Northern Sinfonia *should* be depended more than anything on what sort of music it wanted to perform; what size the orchestra could be related more to finance. To be purely a string orchestra would be too restrictive of repertoire. To be a full 'symphony' orchestra – in late nineteenth century terms, with massed strings, full complement of brass, etc. was not necessarily desirable on artistic grounds. Basically a body of strings with a modest complement of woodwind and brass would have the capacity for a substantial and varied repertoire: from the music of the Baroque (and earlier) to selected works from the nineteenth and twentieth centuries, including most of the great 'classics' of Vienna in its heyday. There would also be the potential for new commissions appropriate to the Orchestra's forces – with an emphasis on works featuring Orchestra members as concerto soloists. While 'expansion' has featured on many a Northern Sinfonia management agenda, it was wisely never thought of as a priority.

There were precedents for this approach in the Stuttgart Chamber Orchestra; and in this country, the Boyd Neel,

Jacques, and Lemare Orchestras of the 1930s. Among these, the Sinfonia remains distinct as the first chamber orchestra with permanent salaried players. The evident popularity of the smaller ('chamber') orchestra gives credence to the claim that such forces can give a cleaner, more attractive sound; indeed for much of the Classical repertoire, a modest orchestra – similar in size to that in use in Haydn's or Beethoven's day – is properly applauded as a more authentic approach to performance.

However, the audiences of the North East expected value for their money. 'Most engagers wanted programmes including trumpets and timpani...' it was noted in the Finance Minutes (12 May 1981) – which also meant bringing in more string players to balance the fuller brass. The contrast in numbers this produced was a considerable financial factor: it was reckoned '30 players would suffice for Mozart and chamber concerts, [but] 60 for the Orchestra's principal engagements in Newcastle and Middlesbrough.' (*The Guardian* 26 Nov 1960)

Aside from the financial strain, it was apparent an augmented orchestra, with extra players brought in, needed more rehearsal time and risked a less polished performance. As Michael Hall had earlier pointed out, it was better to concentrate on becoming a *permanent* chamber orchestra since, 'the cost of extra players for large concerts could be prohibitive and the standard of playing also be affected.' (*The Journal* 26 May 1961)

The point was worth re-emphasising in 1988 when it was stated 'the Orchestra will specialise in music suited to its size and character, bringing in other instruments on a limited and selective basis according to the requirements of this repertoire.' (Corporate Plan 1988–91)

## 'The advantage of permanency'

Retaining a core of players on a contract basis was an important step forward. An orchestra with a stable composition, regularly playing together, was essential if Northern Sinfonia was to develop its own artistic voice and continue to improve the co-ordination of its playing:

> 'The advantages of permanency to an ensemble of this size are very great. It is inevitable that the Orchestra should draw largely for its repertoire on the works of the eighteenth century, and the opportunity of constant rehearsal – day in day out – gives to the group a chance to achieve the style and polish particularly important in such music.'
> (NS prog. 17 Mar 1962)

The core orchestra of 1961 was in some ways a rather spartan force, with no more than 19 permanent players: a body of strings, two oboes and two horns – reflecting the essential forces for much of the Baroque repertoire. In 1962 a flute, two bassoons and a harpsichord player were added to the forces. Later still, a clarinet was brought in – but the harpsichord post was temporarily suspended.

As the orchestra gradually increased its contract players from 19 in 1961 to 23 in 1965 to 28 in 1991, with 37 as a realisable target, a significant issue became that of maintaining the balance between sections of the orchestra. Their proportions are expressed by a formula, e.g. for the Stuttgart Chamber Orchestra: 4, 4, 3, 3, 1 plus two oboes plus two horns, where the first five figures represent the strength of the strings (1st violins, 2nd violins, violas, cellos, and double-bass, respectively). For the Sinfonia in 1967, the string proportions were 4, 4, 3, 3, 1; while in the 1980s, a target of 8, 6, 4, 4, 2 was set, plus two flutes, two oboes, two clarinets, two bassoons, and two French horns – though finances did not at that time permit a sixth second violin or a second flute.

In the 1992–93 financial year, Enhancement Funding from the Arts Council permitted expansion to 37 players, but in practice a full complement was not always in place: in 1994 four vacancies meant an actual playing strength of 33. Nonetheless the current ideal is pitched at: strings 8, 6, 4, 4, 2; two flutes, two oboes, two clarinets, two bassoons; two horns, two trumpets and one timpanist.

Size of course is no true indicator of quality, and Northern Sinfonia's growing reputation, at home and abroad, fully justified its sense of being, 'an international orchestra based in Newcastle' – a status achieved by remaining a characteristic chamber orchestra and benefiting from the flexibility that a moderate establishment brings with it.

## The conductors and conducting

The conductor, it may be, is best thought of as a pivot. He is the centre point between the composer and the sound, and between the orchestra and the audience, as he is (in the artistic sphere) between the orchestra and the management. In football terms, he would be like a manager expected also to lead the team on the pitch (and win every match). The conductor has the main say in the shaping of the orchestra's programme, and so a permanent conductor has often taken the title of 'Artistic Director' in Northern Sinfonia's case, implying, 'an overall responsibility for maintaining the artistic profile of the orchestra.' (*Artistic Policy* 28 Jan 1993).

The Artistic Director will play the major role in setting the orchestra's style (and image) and in shaping its musical voice; his many jobs will include participating in

> '... the selection of guest conductors, soloists and orchestral personnel and the monitoring of orchestral standards... the choice of repertoire, including the commissioning of new works.' (*Friends News* Jan 2002)

He necessarily bears much of the responsibility for a concert's success; if, in addition, he is able to bring to the job contacts that lead to prestigious concerts, recordings and tours, so much the better!

In a chamber orchestra, the conductor does not always play quite the expected role: 'he is in essence a co-ordinator,' Boris Brott opined; 'he must accept the individual qualities of each of the players.' (BBC film *Workshop*, 1966). In eighteenth century performances the principal first violin ('concert master') would likely direct the orchestra, and in a concerto the soloist might well double as player and director of the orchestra. The Sinfonia were early to take up such authentic (and challenging) practices – Andor Foldes doubled as piano soloist and director of the orchestra in a Northern Sinfonia concert of 1961. Subsequently, notable soloists have often been selected as conductors: Tamás Vásáry (pianoforte), Heinrich Schiff (cello), and Thomas Zehetmair (violin).

However, Northern Sinfonia never saw itself as an exclusively Baroque/Classical Orchestra, and it is a matter of fine judgement how far into the nineteenth century the role of soloist/director can be taken. Such ventures depend a lot on the musical maturity of soloist and orchestra alike, and the Sinfonia has not yet reached breaking-point!

## Michael Hall as conductor

In 1960, Michael Hall commented on the role of conductor:

> 'Being an orchestral conductor is not like being an officer in charge of troops, or a business executive imposing discipline. The technique is different in that you set out to win the support of the players by the exercise of your own imaginative ideas. You persuade them to work with you.' (*The Journal* 18 Nov 1960)

The talent required is considerable, since (Michael continued) the conductor had to impart to the orchestra, as though, 'by some sort of telepathy,' the feelings of the composer, whose moods might alter violently from bar to bar.

Michael Hall at rehearsal

'Mr Michael Hall is a conductor who evidently believes that the work should be done at rehearsal, for his manner on the rostrum is restrained and he makes no attempt to render his share in the proceedings obtrusive. That he is a sound musician is shown by the results he achieves...' (Archive 5/1/1)

While the *Evening Chronicle* commented:

'Michael Hall's conducting was highly efficient without the spectacular excesses of some of his showman colleagues.' (Review of first concert, 23 Sep 1958)

A sociable figure, at a time when the Orchestra was necessarily intimate, and bound together with the sense of a new and promising venture – of a venture that had to be made to work – Michael had the right contacts, energy and skills to guide the Orchestra through the critical early years and instil it with purpose. Not forgetting his considerable programming acumen.

'A Mozart symphony can express some fantastic emotions in as little as eight bars and the conductor has to make these emotions so vivid that the orchestra – and the audience – sense the full expression.' (*ibid.*)

Interpreting is almost too gentle a term for this: a conductor cannot be unaware of the need to give a personal performance, almost a display. As Michael Hall put it:

'I like acting. One has to, to be a conductor. Good mime and an ability to project something to the orchestra is essential.' (*ibid.*)

His style with the baton was not unduly flamboyant however, as Arthur Milner of *The Journal* noted:

After six seasons with the Orchestra (later engagements sometimes did not exceed three years), it could be argued that change was beneficial if the players were to learn more and the Orchestra as a whole move on to new challenges. Michael Hall did not disappear from Northern Sinfonia's ken in 1964 – he continued as guest conductor after that and returned for landmark concerts such as the 30th 'birthday' concert in 1988. Overall his involvement in conducting decreased after leaving Northern Sinfonia – his main work lay with the BBC, and, later, as a university lecturer. He now lives in busy retirement in France, an admired author of books on music, with new projects always in mind.

*Rudolf Schwarz*

## Rudolf Schwarz and Boris Brott

When Boris Brott, aged 19, from Canada, and Rudolf Schwarz, veteran conductor of the BBC Symphony Orchestra, arrived to take over, in tandem, a greater contrast between two people or two approaches to music could not have been devised. If it were a matter of the sheer number of newspaper column inches, Brott would be by far the winner, amongst all Northern Sinfonia's conductors; his popularity with the press and their younger readers (including 'I love Boris' sweaters and badges) – aided by the aura of all things Transatlantic prevailing at the time – may obscure the value of the many interesting projects he devised for the Orchestra and yet, it was surely Schwarz who had the more enduring effect, who taught the Orchestra more and formed their style with his admirable experience of the classics of all eras.

Not that Brott, young as he was, was unqualified for his role: he had studied in Canada under Paul Monteux and acted as assistant conductor of the Toronto Symphony Orchestra. In Newcastle, he obtained a key role for Northern Sinfonia in a new music series on Tyne Tees Television, devised many interesting concerts, and arranged Northern Sinfonia's first LP recording opportunities. As conductor, his style was mobile, expressive, almost balletic; his aim to achieve, 'an attitude of co-operation – of intense enthusiasm.' (BBC film *Workshop*, 1966) But for all his good intentions, he outwore Sir Humphrey Noble's initial goodwill, and proved impatient of the exacting demands of orchestral routine.

Rudi Schwarz was by no means so charismatic a figure: as conductor his arm gestures were rather cramped due to the grim legacy of a shoulder-blade broken in Auschwitz – but this did not prevent clear indications and strong rhythm. Steeped in the authentic 'Classical' tradition (he was born in Vienna in 1905 and was joint conductor with Josef Krips at the State Theatre, Karlsruhe, 1927–1933),

his concerts reflected the richness of this repertoire, with a fine feeling for the music of Richard Strauss whom at one time he studied under. At best, his conducting was bold and inspirational, but he could be voluble and excitable, and had little time for the 'avant-garde' of 'Schoenberg, Webern, Maxwell Davies...' as he put it.
(Man. Mins 3 Dec 1963)

Noting his reservations about certain modern music and his disinclination (though a former conductor of the National Youth Orchestra) to conduct concerts in schools, Northern Sinfonia management were content that, 'he would bring a name to the Orchestra and he is a good trainer.' (*ibid*.) His work as re-builder of the post-war Bournemouth Municipal Orchestra was admirable, and it could well be hoped he would have a comparable, positive impact in Newcastle. As George MacDonald (clarinet) reflects: 'He made the Sinfonia listen to themselves – blend with each other... he helped form the Orchestra's style and gave them musical discipline.' (Archive 7/8).

Northern Sinfonia violinist Martin Hughes felt, 'he learnt most from Rudolf Schwarz whose sense of rhythm, structure and tempo was exceptional.' (*Friends News* Mar 1998) Schwarz considered, for example, that the tempos of the movements of a symphony should be related ('a basic pulse running through whole symphony' as Antony Cullen, viola, puts it) and took a stand against phrases being trailed off ('feminine endings') – 'Play what is there!' was Schwarz's motto.

His impact was such that in November 1964 the Orchestral Committee wrote to Sir Humphrey, as Chairman:

> 'We, the Orchestra, wish to assure the management of our utmost confidence in Rudolf Schwarz and seek the assurance of the management that his appearance next season will be as frequent as his other commitments permit...' (letter of 18 Nov 1964, Archive 1/2/2)

Their wish was granted, and it was not until 1973 in his late 60s that Rudi Schwarz indicated a need to wind down his commitment to Northern Sinfonia.

## Artistic directors

The choice of conductor – or artistic director, to use the wider title – lies ultimately with the Management Committee, though this is a matter in which the Orchestra is necessarily closely involved (the introduction to Schwarz, for example, originated when David Haslam, Northern Sinfonia flautist, 'jumped aboard his ferocious Norton 650 motorbike and zoomed down to London to beard Rudi in his Putney den.' (*40 Years*) The common aim is always to secure a conductor who would want the sort of music good for Northern Sinfonia.

The successor to Schwarz (from September 1973) was Christopher Seaman – the choice of the management and the Orchestra. After Brott left, David Haslam continued to assist with some of the conducting load, and Neville

*Christopher Seaman*

Marriner (of The Academy of St Martin-in-the-Fields fame) had guest conducted, making a recording with the Sinfonia in 1971. Seaman, though, was thought likeliest to continue the tradition of Rudolf Schwarz. After studying at Cambridge University and the Guildhall School of Music, he had become timpanist for the London Philharmonic Orchestra (a good post to observe the art of conducting from!) and in 1968 was appointed assistant conductor of the BBC Scottish Orchestra. His expertise in percussion gave him a great sense of rhythmical accuracy, emphasised through the use of a big Sir-Adrian-Boult-style baton to conduct with. His first concert with Northern Sinfonia as principal conductor coincided with the debut of The Sinfonia Chorus in Haydn's 'Nelson' Mass, and as Gerald Larner reported in *The Guardian*, 'Mr Seaman's interpretation was a model of classical freshness and clarity.' (10 Nov 1973)

When Christopher Seaman moved on in 1979 (later to take up the conductorship of the Rochester Philharmonic Orchestra in New York), Northern Sinfonia reverted to a dual directorship: the Hungarians Tamás Vásáry and Iván Fischer. Perhaps a change of outlook was in order: two musicians of such high standard were well-qualified to provide the Orchestra with new inspiration. Of the two, Fischer tended to concentrate on conducting, and was keen to explore the earlier music of the Baroque (for example, the work of Biber from seventeenth century Bohemia), while not neglecting Classics and the Modern. In violin player Martin Hughes' words, he was, 'a very interesting musician who experimented in Baroque playing techniques and brought new insights into the Baroque and Classical repertoire.' (*Friends News* Mar 1998) He 'espoused the new Baroque movement and brought a new style of playing to performances of the Baroque repertoire,' as Antony Cullen commented.
(*Friends News* Jun 1998)

*Iván Fischer*

In an interview with *Classical Music*, (16 Feb 1980), Fischer enlarged on his role: 'The main thing is to avoid playing in a way that is based on nineteenth century orchestral practice.' His idea was

> '...to achieve freer rhythmical method which would bring out what [Fischer] calls the "rhetoric" of each phrase, aiming for a lighter, clearer sound which will allow the individual lines of the texture to be separately audible.'

Vásáry was noted particularly for his piano playing, 'first as a child prodigy and then, after years in the wilderness following his departure

*Tamás Vásáry*

from Hungary in 1956, as a rediscovered star.' (Gerald Larner in *The Guardian* 12 Feb 1980). 'A star as a pianist, a democrat as a conductor,' Vásáry served memorably as soloist in many Northern Sinfonia concerts. His recording of the Piano Concertos of Chopin may be cited as an example of his playing at its best – emotionally committed and urgent while showing exactly the right respect for the works' lyrical quality.

Fischer went on to found the Budapest Festival Orchestra in 1983, and was appointed Music Director of the Opéra National de Lyon in 2000.

The appointment of Richard Hickox as Artistic Director in 1982 marked a notable step forwards in the national profile of Northern Sinfonia; he was untiring in obtaining engagements for the Orchestra and promoting recording opportunities, including choral work and opera. He had trained as an organist at Cambridge, and had considerable conducting experience: as master of the LSO Chorus, and founder (1971) and musical director of the City of London Sinfonia. His contacts with UK music festivals and opera directly benefited Northern Sinfonia in terms of festival work, tours and recordings.

Coming to the post after Northern Sinfonia had mounted a number of concerts for strings alone, he opened up the repertoire and redefined the role of Artistic Director. As conductor, his strengths were deemed to lie in choral music and English music of the twentieth century, e.g. Elgar, Vaughan Williams and Benjamin Britten, composers whose work featured in some memorable recordings with Northern Sinfonia. From 1984–88 he conducted the Orchestra in a cycle of Beethoven symphonies, recorded for

*Heinrich Schiff*

ASV (considered more fully under recordings, later). Remembered as, 'a lovely man,' he had a good sense of what would appeal to the public, some tact in the inclusion of modern music in a programme, and exceptional skill as a choral conductor: he seems to have had a real understanding of the human voice and, 'a tremendous ear for the Chorus.'

Next came Heinrich Schiff's tenure as Artistic Director of Northern Sinfonia, 1990–1996. Born in Gmunden, Austria, and trained as a cellist in Vienna, his considerable experience of European orchestras and music made him the ideal complement to Richard Hickox. His many contacts abroad assisted in attracting important soloists to come and play with Northern Sinfonia.

In the 1990–91 *Prospectus*, it was noted that he planned, for the coming season, 'an emphasis on the Viennese Classical repertoire, together with a passionate interest in contemporary music – particularly that of Russia, Poland, Austria and Germany.' In the 1993–94 season we find a creditable mix of Classic and Modern: Saint-Saëns, Falla, Rodrigo, Mozart, Casken, Ruders, Dutilleux, Mahler, Richard Strauss, but above all, Beethoven.

Schiff's expertise with the cello was evident in his role as soloist-director; he played, by preference, a Stradivarius, made in 1711 and known as 'The Mara', though he also has a Montagnana cello from 1739, known, even more romantically, as 'The Sleeping Beauty'. John Casken wrote his Cello Concerto for him.

Intriguingly, this well-travelled personality found the countryside around Newcastle, 'one of the prettiest anywhere, not just the sea and Lake District, but everything about it...' and one of the added pleasures of being with Northern Sinfonia was being enjoined 'to play in small towns.' (BBC *Music* May 1990)

Jean-Bernard Pommier – Artistic Director 1996–99 – studied piano and conducting at the Paris Conservatoire and went on to work with Karajan and the Berlin Philharmonic. Much admired as a pianist – he won a place in the finals of the Tchaikovsky Competition at only 17 – his recordings include the complete sonatas of Mozart and Beethoven as well as well-known piano concertos by Tchaikovsky, Rachmaninoff and Mozart.

He first met Northern Sinfonia at the Prades Festival in southern France, where he arranged a concert for them though he knew the Orchestra only by its reputation at that time. Subsequently he performed the Beethoven piano concertos with the Sinfonia, proving an excellent director from the keyboard and someone who could achieve, 'tremendous rapport with the audience.' (per Noel Broome) He seemed a natural choice to succeed Schiff, and guided Northern Sinfonia in an orthodox path, maintaining a sensible core repertoire. In the 1999–2000 season he contributed three performances to the schedule, playing Saint-Saëns' Piano Concerto no. 2 in G minor and Beethoven's 1st and 5th Piano Concertos.

After Pommier, there was a gap in appointing a music director – the plans for Northern Sinfonia had reached a critical stage, and it was not until 2002 that the situation stabilised sufficiently to make a new appointment appropriate; the successes of the past ensured that the post would go to someone who could combine the roles of soloist and conductor...

## Thomas Zehetmair

Thomas Zehetmair took on the role of Music Director in 2002, being, 'centrally involved in the planning of repertoire, commissions, tours, and the engagement of guest conductors and soloists, orchestral personnel, recordings and broadcasts.' (NS prog. 18 Feb 2004) He has led Northern Sinfonia further afield in the Romantic repertoire, showing how well an orchestra of 40 (or fewer) can deliver major works. A great musician and superb violin player in his own right, he has shown admired skill both in directing from the first violin desk and more formal rostrum conducting, with a natural gift for gesture

*Thomas Zehetmair*

and finding the right 'body language' to elicit the intended response in sound.

His instrument of choice is a Stradivarius of 1692, known as 'The Falmouth'. He has recorded violin concertos by Beethoven, Brahms, Sibelius and Bartók and many more (the conductor for the Bartók being Iván Fischer). As well as a soloist of international status, he is well-known for his chamber music playing, as leader of the Zehetmair Quartet. Their CD of Schumann's first and third Quartets for ECM New Series won the coveted *Gramophone Magazine* award for 'record of the year' in 2003. As the editor enthused, 'It has an immediacy and excitement that really sets it apart from the average chamber music recording.' Significantly, Zehetmair later commented: 'In conducting you have to listen to all the different parts – in quartet playing, it's very delicate – it's good training for conducting.' (pre-concert talk, 18 Feb 2004)

His greatest challenge (and achievement) may prove to be the adventure of conducting Northern Sinfonia in their purpose-built concert hall at The Sage Gateshead.

## The players

Membership of an orchestra is quite properly by audition only. However, as well as seeking players of the highest quality, Northern Sinfonia has been adept in attracting players who stay and serve over a long period, helping build and retain the Orchestra's character, as explained in the magazine, *Music*:

> '... the Orchestra enjoys a strength derived from the unusual loyalty of its many long-term members, and, because it has particularly able players in various principal roles, it is a flexible body, superbly capable in chamber and solo as well as orchestral work.' (May–Jul 2003)

This is surely a major factor in Northern Sinfonia's success – its essentially intimate and flexible character, allowing scope for individual players as soloists, chamber musicians, music teachers, and even as conductors and composers, within the framework of the Orchestra itself. In some sense this reflects the aspirations of the players from early on: 'They *believed* in the Sinfonia, which was small because they wanted to be a chamber orchestra and versatile because they wanted to do lots of different things...' (Tony Froud, Archive 7/9)

An interesting and evocative film, *Workshop*, made by the BBC about Northern Sinfonia in 1966 includes reflections on playing in a chamber orchestra by some of its early members. From Antony Cullen (viola): 'The first pleasure of playing in a chamber orchestra is you get the chance of hearing yourself.' John Williams (oboe) talked of the advantage of 'much more freedom in your own playing' – in the sense of initiative and even responsibility, since, as Norman Horrod (horn) pointed out, 'you simply cannot get away with slack playing in such an ensemble.' Michael Chapman (principal bassoon 1964–79) commented on, 'the advantages of being able to live in the countryside while going to work in a city.' Conductor Boris Brott summarised the ethos of chamber orchestra (no longer, after all, a private aristocratic establishment) as, 'an attitude of mind towards the music by the musicians themselves.'

An orchestra is necessarily a structured body, with players arranged on stage at a series of 'desks' that reflect (to a degree) experience and status. Nonetheless this 1966 film probably does justice to Northern Sinfonia in stressing its relative informality and sociability. At that time the average age of players was under 27.

## Leaders of the orchestra

The importance of the leader of the orchestra goes back to the Mannheim Orchestra of the mid-eighteenth century, when a harpsichord (continuo) player was less likely to give the players their directions than the principal first violin. In the words of an early Northern Sinfonia sleeve-note: 'In Mannheim, at instrumental concerts, the orchestra leader was usually the first violinist, or concert master, and he usually conducted with his bow from the first violin part.' (Hope Sheridan, 1967)

The leader retains a role of much importance today, in terms both of playing skills and leadership skills; a figure whose example helps set the style of playing of the orchestra, and who acts as an essential contact point: helping interpret (as it were) the conductor's intentions to the orchestra and, conversely, often acting as a practical spokesman for the orchestra in processes of consultation.

In considering possibilities for the post of leader in 1958, Michael Hall commented of one applicant (giving us a neat summary of the role of leader in the process):

> 'I'm told that not only is he a good player and leader, but he is also easy to work with and respected by other players – which, if it is true, sums up the ideal leader.' (Archive 7/1)

A Northern Sinfonia programme of 10 June 1964 gives more detail on the role of the leader:

> 'On the face of it his job, like any other principal player's, is to ensure that his section plays with complete unanimity of bowing and phrasing and to play any passage marked 'solo'. However, his influence is much greater than this; his writ will run on all general matters in the other string sections, and in so far as the strings are the basis of the texture, to which the wind is a contrast and adornment, in the wind also. He has a marked effect on the rhythmic response of the orchestra to the conductor: he must have the nerve and experience to follow any gyrating hieroglyphs in the stick. In brief, he must command respect...'

Jack Rothstein    Joseph Segal

A responsible post and one involving a range of skills. The list of Northern Sinfonia leaders has included many notable players: Leonard Friedman in the beginning (1958–59), with Jürgen Hess as his Deputy; then Kenneth Sillito (who later joined the Academy of St Martin-in-the-Fields to become its Artistic Director), Marie Wilson, Michael Jones, Joseph Segal (from the Hallé; sadly he had to retire from Northern Sinfonia after injuries in a car accident); Christopher Hirons, Jack Rothstein of whom Rudolf Schwarz said:

> 'Whether it is attainable or not remains to be seen, but what we are aiming for under Mr Rothstein's guidance is the almost telepathic ensemble-playing of a string quartet so that on the concert platform all we have to think about is the music' (*Prospectus 1970–71* p.9)

There followed the long tenure of Barry Wilde (1971–82), a tactful and good-humoured problem-solver – something of his style of playing can be appreciated in Northern Sinfonia's recording of Grieg's Holberg Suite; and then Bradley Creswick, who served as leader 1984–7, breaking to work as leader of the Philharmonic 1987–91 and of the Royal Opera House Orchestra 1991–94 while Paul Barritt served as leader here 1988–94. Bradley Creswick returned to Northern Sinfonia in 1994. As he put it, 'I've missed the friendliness and wit of the people here.' (*Friends News* Autumn 1994)

One of the regular responsibilities of the leader is to take charge of preliminary rehearsals, the occasions when problems are ironed out and a thorough familiarity with the score established or re-established, prior to the more advanced shaping and interpretation that the conductor proper will want to effect. Depending on the leader's temperament and personality, there may be a part to play in programming and scheduling – advising what can and cannot be achieved; in auditions, and in the general spheres of discipline and quality of playing. In the actual concert, it is the leader who signals the formal tuning of the orchestra, prior to the entry of the conductor; and at the conclusion of a concert it was customarily the leader who shook hands with a soloist, or rose to take a preliminary bow on behalf of the orchestra as a whole; but this brief prominence is but a poor symbol of the important role he or she plays in the wider life of the orchestra, as regards its music, organisational concerns and general welfare.

## Strings

The strings are the heart of the orchestral sound, their singing tone essential to what we think of as 'Classical' and indeed 'orchestral' music. Their combined range – covering easily six octaves – makes them one of the most versatile of the families of instruments, being equally accomplished at carrying the melody (especially so the violin and cello) and providing harmonic texture; impressive in passages of sustained sonorous tone, yet agile enough to handle the fastest of runs and arpeggios.

Significantly, the strings are instruments designed for indoor performances. The number of instruments playing each part needs to be adjusted to suit the size of the hall or the composition being played, providing a basic setting of the overall volume or 'body' of sound. Playing in unison has therefore long been an essential skill for the string player!

In letters of 1958, Michael Hall set down something of his ideas on the kind of string players he was seeking to enlist. They were to be, 'young, keen and malleable, if possible...' and,

> '... ideally I want players who are intensely musical and who play a lot of chamber music. I want utmost flexibility of tone and easier rhythm rather than precision and acrobatics. Above all, I want players who still love music, who want to play better, and don't look on the business as first a job!' (Archive 7/1)

Two possible proportions for the string departments were sketched down at this preliminary stage: type 'A' being 8,6,4,4,2 (being the numbers of first and second violins, violas, cellos, doubles-basses, you will recall); type 'B' being 6,6,4,3,2. Different programmes of music were considered appropriate to the different balance of tone: 'A' emphasising the melody, e.g. for most Mozart, Haydn, Beethoven; 'B' a more consistent harmonic texture appropriate to, e.g. the darker colours of Mozart's G minor Symphony (no. 40) and the harmonies of Bartók and Fauré.

It is not unusual for the balance of strings to be adjusted from concert to concert or even from piece to piece, an indication of the central role they play in the orchestral sound, and notably so in the case of a chamber orchestra.

**The violin**
The violin section is the most prominent among the strings, invariably carrying the main themes in traditional classical composition, and divided into two sections to provide more versatility and emphasis to melody, counterpoint and harmony, in the higher registers.

The prominence of the first violins calls for extreme precision of playing, and makes high demands on players at a physical as well as a mental level. Violinists tend to be a young section, perhaps for this reason. It is to be remembered – for most orchestral players – that training starts as a child when co-ordination and musculature are still formative, and involves a course of some 10–12 years strenuous learning before the hopeful young adult is likely to qualify as even a potential professional orchestral player. If fortunate enough to obtain such a post, high standards of playing have to be maintained throughout a long career. This can only be ensured by constant exercise – the devoted Joseph Segal was said to practise regularly till 2 or 3 in the morning.

Understandably, the quality of player needed for Northern Sinfonia was not always easily found, and when located, was vulnerable to attractive offers from London orchestras – Keith Statham (as General Manager) had to act speedily once to retain a leader of the orchestra attracted by an offer from the LPO. However, there must be advantages to living and working on Tyneside, for the violin section is thankfully well 'manned' and more effective now than ever, with due acknowledgement to the notable proportion of women players in its ranks.

Among its many long-serving members we may mention Rosamund Kitchen: she joined Northern Sinfonia in 1983 as co-principal of the second violins, though she has also played with the first violins when needed, and in the chamber music sphere was a founder member of the (independent) Avison Ensemble. As to 'playing second fiddle', she says:

> 'I really enjoy playing second violin. As such, you are actually part of the harmonic make-up of the music, and feel part of the whole sound, rather than just playing the tune – mind you, we make the most of our tunes when we get them!' (*Friends News* Winter 2002–03)

An interesting experiment occurred in Michael Hall's time when it was decided to investigate the Baroque style of playing the violin. Kenneth Skeaping, father of Sinfonia cellist Adam Skeaping, was an expert on eighteenth century violin playing and demonstrated to the Orchestra some of the early techniques, 'to show the Orchestra how the old instruments were played, the kind of bow that was used, the kind of quality of sound and something about the way they would ornament the music.' (Archive 7/7) This was found to be invaluable guidance, but without the funds to purchase authentic instruments, Northern Sinfonia could not really pursue this intriguing line of development.

Making instruments, of course, is a highly skilled craft, and there is a general consensus that the loveliest violin tone is found in older instruments. An interesting exception to this 'rule' is the violin played by Sylvia Sutton in the 1970s: it was made for her by her father (a former miner and welder, but with a remarkable practical talent for working out 'what made things tick').

'When Jan-Pascal Tortelier was playing with the Orchestra and had heard of the violin, he asked if he could try it. He thought it was a wonderful instrument and said he could quite happily record using it!'
(*Friends News* Sep 1998)

## Viola

Compared to the glamour of the violin, the viola may seem a relatively anonymous instrument, often relegated to an 'in-fill' harmony role in an orchestral score (a legacy of the style of scoring made popular by Johann Stamitz in the mid-eighteenth century). Yet it has a tenor voice of its own, and the fine playing of Roger Best (principal viola from 1961 on) gave rise to the commission of two viola concertos to be played by him with Northern Sinfonia.

Player Noel Broome pointed out that, like Bach and Mozart, it is perfectly acceptable (possibly ideal) to play the viola and be, 'at the centre of the harmony.' While as a solo instrument, it becomes, 'in the hands of a proficient player one of the most beautiful of all instruments, outstanding for the veiled quality of its tone and its richly expressive range.'
(*The Northern Echo* 30 Mar 1979)

A notable early member of the viola corps was Antony Cullen, a friend of Michael Hall from the Royal College days who also served in the demanding role of General Manager 1960–1961 and who continued to play with Northern Sinfonia, as needed, after his formal retirement in 1996. Antony in a sense founded the viola section, as he was playing in the Hallé under Barbarolli when he decided to throw in his lot with Northern Sinfonia, and soon brought with him two other Hallé players, Roger Best and Fred Crawshaw, providing a stable viola section for almost 20 years. In retirement, Antony is still an active player, and helps organise the Newcastle Chamber Music Society.

## Cellos

The noble violoncello is both an effective bass to the string section and fine lyrical instrument in its own right. Its glorious solo capability is not often heard in Baroque music, though it is often required to execute demanding passages of fast-fingering, in parallel to the violins!

One context in which the cello can be heard to its best is in chamber music, where its role as a bass instrument with a lovely higher register for melody is displayed to perfection. Many string players enjoy the chance, within Northern Sinfonia or in groups of their own, to participate in such chamber music work; and though we are mostly concerned here with the story of the Orchestra it is well to remember that chamber music includes some of the greatest works of the famous composers, and in this sense, 'small' has always meant 'special'. As chamber concerts in the region have shown, here are players who can understand the complexities of this special repertoire and work closely together – unconducted – to interpret some of the most challenging works of the masters.

Ruth Bennett, who joined the Orchestra in 1961, and has now retired, still plays in some chamber concerts; she

*Ruth Bennett*

recalls with particular reverence the playing of guest soloist Mstislav Rostropovich. As an encore he might typically play part of a Bach solo cello suite, and Ruth once casually mentioned to a friend in the Orchestra that she would love to hear him play the Bach C major suite, '... and then, one concert he did so (or three movements there from) turning and dedicating it to me!' (Archive 7/8) A pleasant reminder of the essentially graceful manners typical of the most famous of musicians.

**Double-bass**

An octave lower than the cello, the double-bass is not usually reckoned a solo instrument, but is destined to double the part written for the cello, giving depth and resonance to the bass line. The large, dominant sound it engenders means only one double-bass is required to a considerable body of strings, and for many years Northern Sinfonia relied on a single contracted player – Bryan Maynard till 1971, then David Munro (to 2003); in 1983, a permanent second double-bass was appointed.

An early member of the team, Bronnie Best, commissioned her own double-bass: She talks eagerly about the instrument – it was made by Northern Sinfonia's lead double-bassist, Bryan Maynard, from 200-year-old sycamore and elm. 'I chose the colour myself – it's much lighter than most. It took Bryan about two and a half years to make and it cost me £400 (in 1971 money). Also it has five strings, which is unusual.' (*The Journal* 24 Sep 1971) Five strings means less span is needed to reach the full range of notes: a scale that looks simple on a violin can be quite an athletic challenge on a double-bass!

David Munro retired in 2003 after some 30 years with Northern Sinfonia (but still plays with them!). He was originally set for a career in the law, when he switched to playing double-bass with the City of Birmingham Symphony Orchestra. After seven years there, he took the opportunity to become principal bass player with

*David Munro*

Northern Sinfonia, with the added attraction of making Newcastle his family home.

His view on playing double-bass in the orchestra is that it is 'satisfying – you do feel as if you're underpinning the whole structure.' (Archive 7/8) Not an ostentatious role, but a very responsible one.

## Woodwind

The woodwind comprises the oboe family (with double reed, including the cor anglais and bassoon), the clarinet (with single reed), and the flute, which needs no reed to generate its pure sound. The oboe and flute have prototypes far back in history whereas the clarinet was developed around 1700 and took nearly a century to become a standard member of the orchestra. In the nineteenth century systems of keys to make a full and easily accessible chromatic scale were added; yet despite their varied origins and tone, the woodwind, as a group, blend well with each other, and form a valuable resource for the composer.

Because of their distinctive and penetrating sound (the oboe's 'A' is the cue to the orchestra to tune up), relatively few woodwind are needed in an orchestra to balance the strings. As though to make up for this, they often have notable solo passages, and a body of chamber music exists that calls for woodwind alone.

In the early seasons, the string section had the first claim on Northern Sinfonia's funds, and it is as well that many Baroque scores only call for a pair of oboes (plus perhaps flutes and bassoons) which conventionally doubled the string parts. A more independent role for the woodwind developed during the eighteenth century, and a typical early nineteenth century score will call for full double woodwind (two flutes, two oboes, two clarinets and two bassoons). In response to these varying needs, Northern Sinfonia's woodwind section has been 'built up' gradually over the years, but has benefited from the experience of some long-serving members – David Haslam (flute), Ron Thorndycraft (bassoon), Colin Kellet (oboe) and George MacDonald (clarinet); and distinguished players like Tony Camden (oboe) and Michael Chapman (bassoon). George MacDonald, from Canada, played in the very first Northern Sinfonia concert; he features as soloist in several Northern Sinfonia recordings. David Haslam studied flute, piano and composition at the Royal Academy of Music; he became principal flute in the Scottish National Orchestra, then joined the Sinfonia as principal flute in 1962, serving also as associate conductor from 1966 (and occasionally as arranger and composer), though now retired. His thoughts on the design of the flute appeared in a Northern Sinfonia newsletter (ca. 1975):

*George Macdonald*

'Of course all flutes used to be wooden, but nowadays there are many more metal ones... The big thing about a wooden flute as far as David Haslam is concerned is that he is far more satisfied with its tone than he is with the sound which he can produce from any metal flute he has ever tried. David Haslam found ready allies in the Flute Makers Guild in London. He and they are determined to produce a wooden flute as advanced as any metal one, and the technical discussions and experiments to this end will go on for some time yet. Meanwhile, however, they have produced him an instrument which has already stood the severe test of a six-week tour of South America, being subjected to extremes of heat and humidity in Nicaragua and minus zero degrees in Buenos Aires...'

*David Haslam*

The distinctive tones and timbres of the woodwind have been welcome resources to twentieth century composers, and modern composers typically provide more scope for individuality than their Baroque counterparts. We may mention here the impressive performance of Frank Martin's 'Concerto for Seven Winds' (18 February 2004) with flute, oboe and clarinet soloists provided from Northern Sinfonia.

**Brass**

The brass, like the woodwind, has ancient roots, and belongs equally to the world of outdoor music: the trumpet (typical of the Roman world) has military connotations, the horn (typical of the Teutonic world) was the instrument of warning and hunting.

The notes of the harmonic series sufficed for conveying simple signals loudly and clearly; intermediate notes could not be easily produced until valves for horns and trumpets were introduced in the early 1800s – a simplification leading to a popular enthusiasm for brass bands by the middle of the nineteenth century.

Previous to this, the brass were used sparingly in orchestral scores. In the eighteenth century, a pair of horns was the standard, 'to strengthen the fullness of sound,' as Hope Sheridan notes on a Northern Sinfonia sleeve-note (1976). In the Mannheim Orchestra, 'The horns were now decisive in determining the new sound picture and, with their long, sustained tones, also provided a pedal point effect within the orchestra.' The first permanent brass players with Northern Sinfonia were thus horns, appropriate to Baroque scoring.

Hugh Potts was french horn player with Northern Sinfonia from the mid-1970s to the mid-80s – he now plays with the BBC Scottish National Orchestra. He started out studying psychology at Durham University and playing french horn with Northern Sinfonia as a student; on graduating he joined the Royal Opera House Orchestra in London; in 1973 he returned to become principal horn at Northern Sinfonia where he coped so admirably with, 'those perilous and exposed passages that fall to the lot of a principal horn in a chamber orchestra.' (NS prog. 17 Dec 1976) The prominence of the brass in such passages requires the utmost skill and concentration: 'in a chamber orchestra you can't get by [with second-class playing]', as Norman Horrod (who played with Northern Sinfonia in the 1960s) remarked; 'the tiniest details have to be worked at meticulously.' (BBC film *Workshop*, 1966)

*Hugh Potts*

*Horns*

The beautiful tone of the current principal horn, Peter Francomb, will be well known to Northern Sinfonia audiences, and can be appreciated in his tenor horn solo in the Britten 'Serenade' (broadcast by the BBC in 2003).

Despite their expertise in the Baroque repertoire, Northern Sinfonia have never aspired to original brass instruments of the period. The choice may have been aesthetic as much as economic; but there are also good practical reasons. A Northern Sinfonia concert usually includes music from a variety of periods, and it would not be feasible to switch between original and modern style instruments from piece to piece.

This must be hard on the trumpets at times. Of a 1968 Northern Sinfonia concert including Handel's 'Firework Music', trumpeter Norman Archibold gave a sensational report:

> 'Our part is so high and so long that it is very easy to run out of oxygen and to blackout completely. I have experienced a blackout before – it is a very dreamlike sensation, but best avoided. In Handel's day every trumpeter has three stand-ins, so ours is a much tougher performance.' (*The Journal* 30 Oct 1968)

Less frequently used in Northern Sinfonia concerts than the french horns, and used sparingly in most scores, the trumpet player may justifiably feel that their lot is to be either, 'bored stiff or scared stiff!'

An article by John Davies in *New Society* (8 Jan 1976) elaborates on this point:

> 'The strings are organised into rather large sections, which involve numbers of people playing the same part. In contrast, brass sections mainly consist of small groups of individuals, each playing his own part. A purely practical result of this is that the brass form a less anonymous group. An error in the second trumpet part is attributable directly to the player in question.'

Risky though the role may be, Northern Sinfonia has had some excellent – and assuredly error-free – trumpet players, including Norman Archibald, Roger Payne and, now, Richard Martin.

Mention must also be made of Clarence Adoo, who was settling in so well with Northern Sinfonia, 'taking his own infectious enthusiasm for music into countless schools on a variety of educational projects... (as well as being) involved in many community and education workshops.' (brochure, Archive 3/3/22) Tragically, while travelling by car to London in 1995, he was caught up in a near-fatal road accident that left him paralysed from the shoulders down and abruptly ended his career as trumpet player.

A trust was set up to help him finance the many special needs he has encountered since. Ebullient and determined to play his part, Clarence is still a valued contributor to the organisation's educational programme.

*Layton Ring*

## Percussion

Timpani – based on the military kettle-drum – are important in many orchestral scores, though for Northern Sinfonia's needs, a single percussion player has generally sufficed. The drums may not often be called on to speak, but their effect is dramatic indeed when they do, so a first-rate timpanist is essential to any orchestra. In the early seasons, Haydn Hartley and Frederick Crawshaw (also viola player) managed timps and percussion as needed; Layton Ring played harpsichord; though by 1974, Alan Fearon had taken on these responsibilities, and has remained with the Orchestra ever since, not just as timpanist, but as continuo player, and most importantly of all, as chorus master of The Sinfonia Chorus.

The association between Alan and Northern Sinfonia began earlier, in 1968, when he was a music student at the University of Durham, and happened to attend a Northern Sinfonia concert at the City Hall, Newcastle, conducted by Rudolf Schwarz. Rudi remembered Alan from his days with the National Youth Orchestra and invited him to play with Northern Sinfonia. As pianist, timpanist or harpsichord player, Alan's many talents were put to good

*Clarence Adoo*

*Alan Fearon*

use in Northern Sinfonia concerts.

The 'continuo group' comprises cellos, double-bass and harpsichord – their role being to manage the bass line, and in the harpsichord's case to, 'fill in harmony when required,' a practice that had its origin in the need to provide support for passages where a Baroque composer would note down only solo and bass lines, 'figured' to indicate the additional harmony needed. Occasionally a soloist like George Malcolm would conduct from the harpsichord, but for Alan, the instrument is usually a subtly sounding but essential member of the Baroque ensemble.

The piano is generally bracketed with the percussion section, though most likely to be heard as a solo instrument in a concerto. Due to the weight of a grand piano and the risk of damage when moving, an instrument is resident to one location rather than moving round with an orchestra. In our region this was the rule at Middlesbrough, Newcastle, Carlisle and the Westmoreland Hall at Kendal (reckoned particularly good quality). Though not best practice, the grand piano shared by Newcastle concert halls tended to be moved around the city according to need and in 1980 was dropped or jarred during transit, breaking the iron frame. In 1986, John Lill offered to give a recital without fee to enable the Northern Sinfonia to buy its own Steinway, but this ambition has had to be deferred to the twenty-first century, when Imogen Cooper provided the necessary virtuosic skill required to enable the purchase of two Steinways to serve solely at The Sage Gateshead.

## The rehearsal

Having assembled the orchestra, in all its sections, past and present, and its conductors and artistic directors, time must be found for that rather essential matter – *Rehearsal*.

Here the all-important groundwork is done that ensures an effective and creditable performance – which may well come over as a taken-for-granted excellence on the night, but would hardly be so without painstaking preparation.

Considering which, a typical rehearsal may appear a casual affair at first sight. Players arrive singly – in informal dress – to uncase their instruments and limber up. The cacophony that results is unavoidable, if the instruments are to be warmed up and tricky passages practised individually. The preparations might include a pause for orchestra announcements before the leader calls for the formal tuning to the 'A' of the oboe. Perhaps the first half of the rehearsal will be taken by the leader, from among the violins – a running through of the score or at least some main passages, with occasional stops for comment (or queries) on phrasing or emphasis. At longer intervals, breaks are necessary if effort and concentration are to be maintained – the rehearsal may resolve into a sectional rehearsal at these times.

The conductor may only appear at a later stage in the proceedings. His arrival, in turn, will be perfectly unceremonial – greeting many familiar faces in the orchestra perhaps – or signalling the rearrangement of the seating to concert format (for example, if the first and second violins are to sit opposite, in authentic antiphonal mode). The more formal part of the rehearsal then begins, concentrating understandably on imminent concert pieces and especially the prominent passages of a composition – the opening of the first movement of a symphony, the right pace to establish for the slow movement, and so on, with attention to the balance of sections, the dynamics, phrasing, ornaments, and the like. It is for the conductor to indicate the various nuances of

*David Haslam taking a rehearsal*

playing required, and if need be clarify any ambiguities in the notation. A lot depends on the conductor's own thorough knowledge of the score (and especially so when guiding the orchestra through unfamiliar and difficult compositions).

The rehearsal will not have the tension of a public performance; but it aims to resolve any problems or uncertainties in advance, so that the performance proper will be technically unruffled and (by a sort of paradox) spontaneous.

The proportion of time spent on rehearsal is an important consideration. Too full a concert schedule might reduce the time for rehearsal to the detriment of the concerts themselves and risk, 'a totally static orchestra' (Man. Mins 20 Jan 1969) – one that is not preparing new works to play, but relying much on a well-tried repertoire. This is a point well appreciated by the orchestra, though the public may not realise the amount of preparation that a good concert requires. In the current schedule, for example, a main concert lasting up to two hours overall is allotted 15 hours of rehearsal time, in sessions spread over the three days before the concert. A lot of work for the musicians (and the conductor) – but time well spent!

*The Sinfonia Centre in the making*

## The Sinfonia Centre

A real problem in the early years of the Orchestra was the lack of a regular venue for rehearsals. The Quaker Meeting House, the People's Theatre, or the Scout House in Osborne Road might be used – the actual concert venue (possibly far from Newcastle) would be unlikely to be available for anything more than an afternoon rehearsal before the concert proper. With some justice it was said, 'A rehearsal centre may not sound very thrilling, but it really is at the heart of all the public activities...' (*Prospectus* 1977–78)

In 1974 it was noted:

> '... the behind-the-scenes working conditions during the many hours of rehearsal have become more and more of a problem. The limited number of halls that can be hired for rehearsals are mostly all deficient in some way for the Orchestra's needs. Some have poor lighting, some poor heating, several both. Others have no loading access for large instruments, and frequently it becomes a headache to find anywhere at all for Orchestra rehearsals.

The management committee of the Northern Sinfonia Concert Society therefore decided that the only solution was to acquire premises for the Orchestra and, after investigating existing buildings, it became clear that the only solution would be to build.' (NS prog. 26 Feb 1974)

The happy result was The Sinfonia Centre at Jesmond Vale with its custom-made rehearsal space (the 'Henry Wood Hall') – first used for rehearsal on 5 March 1975. It may seem an odd priority that so much effort should be put into building a rehearsal facility rather than a concert hall – but concert venues in Newcastle were not lacking, and as explained in a programme of December 1976,

> '... the orchestral working conditions which the Centre now provides are reflected in the Sinfonia's playing wherever it performs, so that the rehearsal centre is of more advantage to all the Sinfonia's audiences than a concert hall in one place would be.'

It served admirably as rehearsal space (and offices) for over 20 years, and proved a most convenient location for players who lived or came to live in the pleasant surrounds of Jesmond and Gosforth. However, the Orchestra moves on, and in April 2002, with allegiances shifting to the south side of the river, rehearsals and offices were moved to Gateshead Old Town Hall ('GOTH'), a memorable Victorian building of 1868, situated on the brow of the hill overlooking the Tyne and the steadily growing new home of the Orchestra, The Sage Gateshead.

*Boris Brott and Northern Sinfonia at the Old Assembly Rooms, Newcastle*

# Chapter Three
## *The concert*

*'The chemistry of the concert hall, that magic bond of sympathy between artists and audience, the joy of seeing as well as hearing the re-creation of great works – not the most glittering performance on* Third Programme *or records can beat it.'*

Margaret Brittain, in Archive 5/1/14 (1962)

### The live option

Without an audience – to state the obvious – there can be no concert (in the sense of a live, interactive performance). The point and purpose of the players' skill and the concentrated work in rehearsal is to share the music; only then can the classics be said to be brought fully to life; and just as the orchestra itself needs to feel as one, so too a successful concert implies a bond with the audience that brings them into the magic circle. 'Precious and indispensable,' Jean-Bernard Pommier termed this sense of mutual collaboration and music-sharing. (*Prospectus* 1996–97)

So how can you best please the audience and bring them most readily into a sense of participation? The answer, some may say, is to play well-known pieces that are recognised and appreciated. What this risks, though, is the narrowing of an already select 'canon' of classics. If a conscious effort were not made to broaden the repertoire – by exploring more fully the work of the masters and their contemporaries, and by introducing new compositions – programming would become so predictable as to discourage even the most ardent of concert-goers. The task falls on the programme designer (alias artistic director) who will need to take a long-term view if the repertoire presented to the public is not to repeat itself unduly.

Asked how he constructed a 'typical concert programme', Michael Hall replied:

> 'Firstly, a box office draw – something like Beethoven's Second Symphony. Then a work of the same period to complement it, perhaps a Haydn overture. Thirdly, a contemporary work, so new that no-one will have heard it before. Lastly a work which the audience may be vaguely familiar with and want to hear again – he suggested the Gabrieli Canzoni.' (*Evening Chronicle* 2 Jan 1963)

In fact, the very first concert played by Northern Sinfonia, on Wednesday 24 September 1958, featured an attractive, well-balanced, if fairly traditional line-up:

> Mozart Symphony no. 38 in D ('The Prague')
>
> Schumman Cello Concerto in A m
> (Joan Dickson, soloist)
>
> Beethoven Symphony no. 2 in D

– but there was variety a-plenty to come in that first season. Each of the six Newcastle concerts of 1958–59 included a soloist in a concerto or similar work. As to scope, on a crude head-count, there were seven pieces by Mozart, three by Beethoven, two by Haydn, and a single work each by Bach, Bartók, Berlioz, Falla, Gabrieli, Mahler, Rossini, Schubert, Schumann, and Wagner. The weight is in the Classical period, but with an interesting mix of later nineteenth and twentieth century music.

The reaction in the press to the first season was favourable, but not uncritical. Of the very first Northern Sinfonia concert, the report in the *Evening Chronicle* stated:

> 'At Newcastle's City Hall last night Michael Hall introduced the City's new and only classical orchestra to an enthusiastic audience… There were some very audible lapses by the brass, the timpani were at times too strong, and there was some hesitation from the strings in the finale of Beethoven's Second Symphony. However, the Orchestra as a whole played with a keen, musical understanding and remarkable sensitivity. It had a brilliant leader in Jürgen Hess.' (23 Sep 1958)

Not bad, surely, for a newly formed chamber orchestra on its first outing, and critical reaction warmed as the season progressed to what no doubt was an increasingly experienced style of performance:

> 'Michael Hall's Sinfonia Orchestra proved itself a mature ensemble of first-class musicians in its third concert at the City Hall last night. The few rough edges which had previously been noticeable have gone and extremely polished professionalism now combines with musicianship to give Tyneside an excellent classical orchestra of its own.' (T. Bergman in the *Evening Chronicle* Jan 1959)

The hard work put in must have been appreciated: a concert of 11 February 1959 drew an audience of nearly 2,000. Plans for the next season (1959–60) permitted an expansion of scope, made possible by the alliance with Tyne Tees Television. There were now seven Wednesday Symphony Concerts, seven Sunday Promenade Concerts, both at City Hall, plus 14 concerts in Carlisle, Darlington, Middlesbrough, and Sunderland. A 'circuit' was being established, so that a group of concerts could be re-played at key regional centres. This idea of a set of 'core' concerts in the region has remained basic to Northern Sinfonia's planning to the present day.

There might occasionally be a specific structure to the programming. In the 1963–64 *Prospectus*, Sir Humphrey Noble announced:

> 'Last season's programmes gave prominence to the works of Mozart. In the forthcoming season… the emphasis will be on Haydn, and all the symphonies known as the first "Salomon" Set will be performed.'

While for 1964–65, with the help of NEAA grants, Northern Sinfonia was able to invite as soloists a very impressive line-up: Igor Oistrakh, Paul Tortelier, Vladimir Ashkenazy, John Ogden and Moura Lympany.

If, briefly, we move ahead to the 2003–04 season, to compare preferences in programming, we find due respect for Bach, Haydn, Handel, Mozart, Beethoven; with a notably stronger proportion of twentieth century music, including many less familiar voices – Christian Darnton, Gerald Barry, Roberto Gerhard, Howard Ferguson, James MacMillan, etc.

Though the advantages of Northern Sinfonia might seem to lie with Baroque music, and authentic-scale performances of the Classical giants, it has consistently been recognised that variety and versatility are priorities, both for the sake of the audience and the artistic integrity of the Orchestra. As stated at a Management Committee meeting of 15 April 1987, 'One of [the Orchestra's] tenets was a balanced, broad repertoire,' and its aim – to 'specialise in non-specialisation.'

## Planning for diversity

Some interesting reflections on practical diversity in programme planning are made in the 1992 Northern Sinfonia publication, *Inside Story*. There it is pointed out that balance must not only apply to each concert in itself but be reflected in the season as a whole, to establish

> '... the mix of great classics and interesting rarities, the ratio of accepted historical masterpieces to challenging new compositions, and the balance between solo concertos and works for the Orchestra alone...'

A pleasing example of balance within a concert was given at City Hall on 18 February 2004 (Thomas Zehetmair conducting): each half contained one Baroque and one Modern work – Handel/Martin, Bach/Stravinsky; the works by Handel, Martin and Bach were concertos, which in their structures exemplify the theme of contrast; while overall diversity was provided by the different orchestral forces required in each piece – strings for the Bach, wind soloists in the Martin. Together it presented a fascinating cross-section of the orchestral repertoire.

Careful planning of this order is both an art and a science. Artistic policy, *Inside Story* points out, involves both practical and aesthetic considerations. The size of the orchestra is one factor, but choice of works depends equally on their displaying 'the requisite musical and intellectual rigour, the requisite musical and emotional content, or the requisite skill in construction.' Sizeable choral works are occasionally tackled, like the Brahms Requiem, but within limits: it was necessary recently to decline politely on the grounds of size and economics a suggestion from a member of the public that the Carlisle series include Wagner's 'Ring Cycle'.

Since those involved often have to work up to three years ahead in planning, there is the added dimension of trying to predict how public favour will change in the meantime. Could there be an easier way? In 1965, 'Mr Schwarz particularly asked for suggested works for performance next season from the members of the Music Panel, members of the Orchestra and any amateurs who wished to do so.' (Exec. Mins Feb 1966) In a sense, this democracy of choice has come about, and at home, one can select whichever CD takes one's fancy. At a public concert the choice is made for you; but it should be a consolation that it is an informed choice, in which the audience, the music critics of the press, scholarly opinions and 'fashions' of the day will all play an indirect role. Whether an individual programme appeals or not, be assured a great deal of thought will have been put into the selection of music presented to the public!

## Ancient and modern

From its inception, Northern Sinfonia established a tradition of featuring twentieth century music in its programming. This has been realised, and continues, with a notable list of premières and commissions for new work, as well as a concert series devoted to modern music.

An important attempt at introducing new compositions to the public was made by Michael Hall in the 1963–64 season in a series of 'Connoisseur Concerts', a phrasing which wisely rewarded the smaller numbers of the public willing to give an ear to 'ultra-modern' music in the 1960s. Sir Humphrey Noble's rather cautious announcement of it ran:

> 'A new feature will be the Connoisseur Concerts at the King's Hall which will include modern music of a kind that does not easily appeal to our usual City Hall audience.' (*Prospectus* 1963–64)

However, with ample rehearsal time at their disposal (once the principle of permanent players had been established), there was no reason Northern Sinfonia could not tackle some more difficult modern music. Beside the precedent of the 'Musica Viva' concerts in Vienna, there was the BBC's own Thursday 'Invitation Concerts' which mixed old and new compositions; Michael Hall followed that pattern in including works by Schoenberg, Alexander Goehr and Peter Maxwell Davies alongside Dunstable and Gabrieli, etc. As bassoon player Ron Thorndycraft wrote:

> 'The concerts had been mostly of modern music but with some early music, both genres severely neglected at that time. The Connoisseur Concerts served to attract national attention to the newly-founded Northern Sinfonia Orchestra with BBC broadcasts and national newspaper coverage.' (Archive 7/2)

However, audience numbers in the concert hall were not so encouraging and Northern Sinfonia's Connoisseur series ended in 1966. As an article by Arthur Milner in *The Journal* tactfully put it:

> 'The policy of the Orchestra has been to include among its items as much novelty as it dare risk, but its efforts in this direction have necessarily been restricted by considerations of financial returns.' (19 Jan 1963)

In 1983, in conjunction with the BBC (plus a grant from the Musicians' Union) a revival of Michael Hall's concept took place under General Manager Martin Manasse's title of 'Contact Concerts', 'a series of concerts created, introduced and played by members of the Orchestra' (*Friends News* Dec 1985) – with a new dimension of informality and an after-concert mingling of musicians and audience. A second series was warranted, this time with a themed programme: the three concerts were 'Under Northern Skies' (a programme linking composers from Newcastle and Scandinavia), 'Pieces of Eight' (a truly amazing sequence of octets from Russia, England, Mexico, Sweden, France and Norway) and with the help of The Sinfonia Chorus: 'Auf Liedersingen Pet!' (Note the pun!) Presentations featured introductions by the players themselves, 'informal, often humorous, occasionally analytical, generally informative and enthusiastic.' The venue varied between the Playhouse, the Polytechnic (now Northumbria University) and Newcastle University, with some at Darlington Arts Centre.

The Contact Concerts continued for two more series, including a notable performance of Chou Wen Chung's 'Sextet', the UK première of Turkish composer Ahmed Adnan Saygun's First Symphony, and a concert to celebrate composer David Blake's 50th birthday.

By the 1990s, no one could deny that 'modern' music had achieved a secure place in Northern Sinfonia's programming, a tribute both to the perseverance of the artistic directors and the growing awareness and enthusiasm of the audiences.

A summary in an Arts Council report on Northern Sinfonia in 1994 gives the following statistics for works performed:

|                          | 91–92 | 92–93 | 93–94 |
|--------------------------|-------|-------|-------|
| Works written since 1982 | 25    | 6     | 12    |
| Works commissioned       | 2     | 1     | 2     |
| First performances       | 2     | 1     | 2     |
| Works written 1945–82    | 21    | 28    | 9     |
| Works written 1900–45    | 98    | 93    | 61    |
| Works written before 1900| 238   | 206   | 174   |

(ACGB Appraisal, Archive 3/2/25)

While the emphasis remained on the Classics, it is notable that over a third of the works performed were twentieth century compositions.

This initiative was also reflected in the programming of a new specialist ensemble drawn from Northern Sinfonia players and named 'Vaganza' (after a composition by then Composer in Association, John Casken). Launched in 1998 with a concert at Spitalfields Festival in London, Vaganza was 'dedicated to the regular performance of major twentieth century classics, revisiting exciting contemporary repertoire and introducing challenging new work.' (Archive 2/11/4)

Ilan Volkov, John Casken and Baldur Brönnimann were conductors at these concerts of twentieth century live music, 'with a cutting edge'. Composers featured included Elliott Carter, Morton Feldman, Edgar Varèse, and John Adams; the ensemble could include piano, harp, harmonium, alongside the expected orchestral instruments.

Though Vaganza no longer functions as a group, new initiatives have taken its place. A series, 'The Late Mix', recently at All Saints, Quayside, has featured many modern works including pieces by John Cage, Pierre Boulez, Judith Weir, Deirdre Gribbin, John Casken, and more, continuing a drive to expand the available repertoire that has been a concern of Northern Sinfonia since its earliest days.

## Commissions

If an orchestra has a responsibility to tackle new trends in music, it also, arguably, needs to acknowledge the needs of the contemporary composer, by premièring new works and commissioning new compositions – for without this encouragement the repertoire for the future would be sadly diminished. Opportunities to hear their work is especially important for new, untried composers – and in 1988 the Sinfonia vowed to work, 'to identify outstanding composers early in their careers.' (NS Corp. Plan 1988–91)

Between 1967 and 1983, on average, Northern Sinfonia commissioned one new work a year – with the help of funds from the Arts Council of Great Britain, Northern Arts, the Calouste Gulbenkian Foundation, and others. Outside funding is indispensable, for orchestra budgets are tight, yet the composer has to have the means to devote time to a composition and its realisation.

An early example was the 'Introduction and Allegro' by David Barlow (a young lecturer at King's College, Newcastle). For the 1960–61 season, works were commissioned from Gordon Jacob and Alan Rawsthorne – the initiative in this case came from Sir Humphrey Noble, not Michael Hall. Gordon Jacob's 'Northumbrian Overture' was based on folk tunes taken from W. G. Whittaker's collection of 'North Countrie Ballads, Songs and Pipe Tunes', and proved a suitable work for both core and children's concerts.

In 1967, an unusual and adventurous commission was John Dankworth's 'Escapade' (for jazz instrumentalists, continuo and chamber orchestra), premièred at the Durham Twentieth Century Music Festival – then taken on tour with another Dankworth piece, and culminating in a concert at the Queen Elizabeth Hall (QEH), London with the addition of a third piece by Dankworth. However, the initiative received disappointing public support; perhaps they were confused by the presentation of jazz in a classical context. If so, they missed the chance to witness a rare appearance of James Galway playing flute with Northern Sinfonia.

A number of commissions were concertos especially designed to feature Northern Sinfonia players as soloists. These included two viola concertos written to be performed by Roger Best (principal violist 1961) by Sir Malcolm Arnold and Richard Rodney Bennett. John Joubert wrote a bassoon concerto for Michael Chapman and the Poul Ruders 'Anima' (Cello Concerto no. 2) was composed for Heinrich Schiff to play as soloist/director in 1994.

Other commissions have included: David Lumsdaine 'Sunflower' (1976), David Blake 'From the Mattress Grave' (1979), William

*John Dankworth and Cleo Laine in concert*

Mathias Concerto for Horn and Orchestra (1983), Edward Cowie Harp Concerto (1986), John Woolrich 'Vaucanson's Machine' (1987), Philip Cashian 'Saint Margaret and the Devil' (1995), Diana Burrell Clarinet Concerto (1996), David Blake 'The Griffin's Tale' (1996), Piers Hellawell 'Drum of the Näjd' (1997), Judith Bingham Bassoon Concerto (1998), and recently, a new composition by Deirdre McKay (Young Sinfonia Composer in Association) premièred by the Young Sinfonia at a Holocaust Memorial Concert in 2003.

We must also mention the important role Northern Sinfonia has played in premièring new (though not commissioned) works such as John Woolrich's 'Songbook II' (1985). Also, the year 1966 embraced no fewer than three premières: Wilfred Mellers' Magnificat, Nicholas Maw's Sinfonia, and Graham Whettam's Sinfonia Concertante (with notable roles for the woodwind section and the harpsichord).

It is an impressive list, which continues today with works from Sir Peter Maxwell Davies (now Master of the Queen's Music), Jonathan Dove, John Woolrich, David Lang, Piers Hellawell and John Casken.

*John Casken*

## John Casken

A long-standing relationship developed between Northern Sinfonia and composer John Casken (since 1992, Professor of Music at the University of Manchester). Born in Barnsley in 1949, John studied composition at the University of Birmingham with John Joubert and Peter Dickinson. He was then awarded a British Scholarship to study with Andrzej Dobrowolski in Warsaw in 1971, a time when he developed an enduring interest in the music of Polish composer Witold Lutoslawksi, with whom he formed a strong and personal association.

In the early 1980s, John came to the North East as a Lecturer in Music at the University of Durham, and it was at this time that members of Northern Sinfonia recorded his 'Firewhirl' for soprano and seven instruments, on the Wergo label. John conducted and the soprano soloist was Teresa Cahill. In the mid-80s the Orchestra performed two of his concertos, prior to performing the world première of 'Maharal Dreaming' at a 1989 concert in Darlington (conducted by Ronald Zollman).

It was this work, commissioned by Northern Sinfonia, that began a more serious association with the composer. It led quite naturally to a formal relationship as the Orchestra's first Composer-in-Association from 1991, an event marked by the Orchestra's Arts Council Tour with Northern Stage of John Casken's first opera 'Golem'. It is from this opera, premiered at the 1989 Almeida Festival and directed by Pierre Audi, that the material for 'Maharal Dreaming' is drawn.

Based on the Jewish legends of Eastern Europe, the story of the Golem tells of a community rescued from persecution by Rabbi Loew of Prague (the 'Maharal') bringing to life an artificial man. Breathing life into the clay, a golem is formed, a super-servant who eventually develops a will of his own, murders one of the community he has been sent to protect, and who has ultimately to be unmade. The composer's own libretto draws on parallel stories and other sources, including scenes from the Old

Testament and Book of Psalms, William Blake and the diaries of Franz Kafka. The music of 'Maharal Dreaming' reworks music from the opera to evoke the thoughts, dreams and premonitions the Rabbi might have the night before his creation was brought to life.

Hence, the work, an orchestral fantasy, was actually an overture for the opera, though for larger forces, performed at a different time and in a different place. The Arts Council tour of 'Golem' was a huge success and launched the composer's association with Northern Sinfonia in a very public manner, helping to fulfil the Arts Council's ambition to

> '... let people see that composers are real, living, breathing people and to encourage the writing of works for the future through hands-on association with an orchestra.' (*Inside Story*)

'Golem' also won the very first Britten Award for Composition in 1990, was recorded for Virgin Classics in 1991, with the original cast, and won the Gramophone Award in the contemporary category in the same year.

The first work that John Casken wrote for the Orchestra under this new Association was his Cello Concerto (1991), commissioned for the Orchestra's Artistic Director at that time, the cellist Heinrich Schiff. Schiff had asked the composer for a concerto that he could direct from the cello, as daunting a task as could face any composer. As well as taking on board the practical implications and the fact that the scoring would need to include chamber-like textures, Casken also developed the idea of weaving his musical ideas around a short haiku-like poem of his own:

> 'Leaves of farewell
> fell wrapped in song
> from winter's tree
> on folds of stone
> through silvern air'

The concerto was premièred at the Schleswig-Holstein Festival that year and later recorded with Heinrich Schiff in the solo role, interacting with the Orchestra in a delicate 'balance of older and newer elements.' The impact of this work was considerable and Northern Sinfonia management noted with approval,

> '... the close relationship which had developed with John Casken over the past few years, and commended the artistic benefits of having such a close-knit partnership with a composer.' (Man. Mins 23 Jul 1991)

Further work in the following years included 'Darting the Skiff' in 1993 – a gift to the Orchestra. This was begun at the Rockefeller Study Center, Bellagio, on the shores of Lake Como in Italy, where the composer was resident in 1992, and the work draws inspiration from the mountainous scenery and the image of boats in movement on the water. Scored for strings alone, it manages to create a remarkable texture of sound by dividing the strings almost to the point of one note per player – what Casken has called, 'three-dimensional chords.' The work was premièred at the 1993 Cheltenham Festival with the composer conducting the strings of Northern Sinfonia in a broadcast on BBC Radio 3.

Although John Casken took up the position of Professor of Music at the University of Manchester in 1992, he has continued to return to Newcastle on a regular basis to work with the Orchestra, both as composer and conductor, including a concert with the Orchestra at the Spitalfields Festival including works by Schnittke and Ruders. Northern Sinfonia welcomed the composer back to Newcastle most recently when it performed 'Darting the Skiff' and 'Maharal Dreaming', as part of 'The Late Mix' series, conducted by Baldur Brönnimann at All Saints Church in November 2003. Casken has also been commissioned to write a new work for the Orchestra with soprano, solo viola, for the season 2005–6.

## Some concerts to remember

Bearing in mind that Northern Sinfonia have performed literally thousands of concerts since 1958, it is an invidious task to give any adequate idea of the quality and range of the music they have presented over the years. A lot of work has been put in by players, conductors and staff to make Northern Sinfonia an orchestra of international status and reputation, and it is necessarily by the standard of concert that this reputation has been gained. Here we can only hope to sample a fraction of this music-making, safe at least in the knowledge that there will be ample opportunity to attend concerts by Northern Sinfonia and enjoy their future music for yourselves, for many years to come.

Among the most memorable concerts for Northern Sinfonia were 'firsts' in London, milestones on the Orchestra's hard-won path to national recognition. George Malcolm helped set up Northern Sinfonia's first appearance at an Albert Hall Prom in 1972 (sold out three weeks in advance!), which featured all of Bach's Brandenburg Concertos, directed by Malcolm from the harpsichord. 'This was quite an occasion,' David Munro (bass) recalled – 'going in for the first time before an audience of 7,000 or 8,000!' (Archive 7/8) (An embarrassment at the time lay in store for bassoon player Ron Thorndycraft who was listening to the Prom on the radio at home, only one bassoon being needed in the Brandenburgs. However, the orchestra list supplied to the audience gave the names of both bassoonists; during the interval the astute promenaders burst out with a chant of 'Where's Ron Thorndycraft?!')

On the 29 April 1983 Northern Sinfonia made its debut at the new Barbican Centre. Myung-Whun Chung conducted a programme comprising Mozart's Symphony no. 25, the E-flat piano concerto K449 (soloist Emanuel Ax), Richard Strauss' Wind Serenade op. 7, and Schubert's popular 3rd Symphony. 'The reception in the hall itself was almost ecstatic,' it was noted (*Prospectus* 1983–84 p. 39), and there was a laudatory review by Edward Greenfield in *The Guardian*. Rudi Schwarz, the conductor to whom Northern Sinfonia owed so much, was in the audience.

While dealing with such memorable performances it seems appropriate to mention the many internationally renowned performers who have worked with Northern Sinfonia...

The Orchestra has been fortunate in its ability to offer roles to some now famous names, early in their careers, Murray Perahia, for example; among guest conductors, Simon Rattle's first recording was with Northern Sinfonia – in Stravinsky's 'Pulcinella'. Vladimir Ashkenazy joined with Northern Sinfonia to give his first concert in the UK after arriving from Russia via Iceland. A rarity of a different sort was when André Previn – contracted to the LSO – gave his only independent concerts outside London with Northern Sinfonia (1971, 1972).

At the other end of a career, the farewell performance of the greatly respected horn player Barry Tuckwell was given with the Northern Sinfonia at the Dolphin Centre, Darlington, in November 1996.

There have been surprises with and for soloists. Yehudi Menuhin arrived expecting to play the Dvořák Violin Concerto to find that Northern Sinfonia had been practising the Dvořák Nocturne for Violin and Orchestra! Undeterred, he conned the score overnight and gave of his best.

Mstislav Rostropovich played the Tchaikovsky Rococo Variations in July 1968 with Northern Sinfonia (Schwarz conducting). The following day he turned up at a fund-raising concert at Rothbury a quartet of Northern Sinfonia members had agreed to do (their nervousness at his

*Mstislav Rostropovich*

arrival can be imagined) – and joined in with a solo of his own, a new Britten cello work – quite a bonus for the audience! His opinion of Northern Sinfonia? 'This is an orchestra of which you should be very proud... I am lost with admiration for its perfect ensemble and its sensitivity.'

For the 30th birthday of Northern Sinfonia, a special guest conductor was arranged: the founder of the Orchestra, Michael Hall, was invited back to conduct a charity concert in aid of the Musicians' Benevolent Fund and the Freeman Hospital Children's Heart Unit Fund. This concert opened the 1988–89 season with performances in Middlesbrough, Newcastle and Carlisle, in a programme including Schubert's 8th Symphony.

Michael Hall was also in attendance for Northern Sinfonia's 'farewell' to Newcastle's City Hall on 3 June 2004. For this, their last concert at the City Hall before taking up residence at The Sage Gateshead, it was elected to repeat the programme of the Orchestra's very first concert in 1958 – Mozart's 'Prague' Symphony, the Schumann Cello Concerto, and Beethoven's Symphony No. 2 in D. It was, Matthew Connolly reported in *The Times*, 'a firecracker of a concert' the splendid playing under Thomas Zehetmair (with Alexander Somov taking the lyrical cello solo) was enthusiastically applauded by a capacity audience, and proper acknowledgement made to the founder – on this occasion seated with the audience, some of whom undoubtedly shared the same concert with him back in 1958.

## Special to the North East

Some of Northern Sinfonia's most enterprising performances have been designed for the enjoyment of the people of the North East, as is only fitting.

The Blaydon Races Centenary Concert of 8 June 1962 came at the climax of a week of celebrations avowedly designed to show Tyneside off to the nation and provide some up-beat publicity for the region. The theme was naturally George Ridley's famous song on the mishaps encountered on a bus journey out to the races in 1862, providing a dual focus on sport and music for what must have been the grandest 'carnival' the region has ever seen.

The celebrations started on Saturday 2 June with a plethora of special events: a Newcastle to Blaydon athletic open-road race, a horse gymkhana at Exhibition Park (with the Northumberland Hussars Band), a Blaydon to Newcastle vintage car rally; a brass band competition (for the 'George Ridley Silver Trophy'), Army displays by Northern Command and Parachute Regiment, and a Grand Civic Dinner Dance in a special marquee at Exhibition Park.

During the week, events included a bicycle race, Old Tyme Music Hall at the Black Bull, Blaydon, a Newcastle and Blaydon schoolchildren's concert, a boat race and a swimming gala (not the same event!), and a motorcycle scramble on the Town Moor – a mix of traditional and modern – no doubt intended to focus attention on the Newcastle of the future as well as the past, and with something of the same civic bravado (dare it be said?) that was helping Northern Sinfonia look toward the future.

On the Friday 8 June came the Blaydon Races Centenary Concert at City Hall, played by the Northern Sinfonia with Michael Hall conducting. The programme was a neat demonstration of the Sinfonia's capabilities and scope, starting with Schubert's 'Unfinished' and Mozart's *Eine Kleine Nachtmusik*, then moving on to local songs (performed by Owen Brannigan with Ernest Lush), and culminating in a massed performance of 'The Blaydon Races' with choir, audience and orchestra.

Well, that was not quite the end – on Saturday 9 June there was the Grand Parade from Newcastle, 'on the road to Blaydon' to re-enact the bus journey of 1862: a marvellous pageant – without (this time) any notable casualties.

On a more compact scale, one of most memorable of Michael Hall's Contact Concerts, at the Connaught Hall of the YMCA, Blackett Street (since redeveloped as Eldon Square Shopping Centre) featured Schoenberg's 'Survivor from Warsaw'.

Though lasting only eight minutes, this piece requires considerable resources: a narrator (the role was taken on this occasion by the well-known Alvar Liddell), as well as men's chorus and orchestra. It is a sharp but redeeming account of the Jewish experience in Warsaw in World War Two written shortly after the War itself. Schoenberg was then living in the United States and was able to contact survivors of the Warsaw Ghetto and incorporate their stories, completing his setting in September 1947.

The selection of this work for performance reminds us of Michael Hall's belief that:

> 'Music is the expression of the innermost feelings, desires and states. It is a kind of catharsis which gives people greater emotional awareness and makes for better self-understanding.' (*The Journal* 18 Nov 1960)

In a different vein, a combination of music and poetry was proposed when the senior North East poet Basil Bunting was invited to read with Northern Sinfonia on the afternoon of 2 June 1966. It almost did not take place. As minutes record:

> 'Mr Bergman [Public Relations] had heard that the Bunting concert in the Concert Series had been changed in favour of a Gilbert & Sullivan concert.
>
> He felt that this was a mistake and that the Bunting Concert would not only be a prestige concert at little expense as there would be no extra players required, but that arrangements were being made to bring a party from London who would fill six extra railway coaches.' (Exec. Mins 16 Nov 1965)

In view of those lucid arguments, the poet's concert at City Hall was reinstated. Bunting read his own work, including part of 'Brigg Flatts', one of the acknowledged masterpieces of twentieth century English writing, interspersed with the Baroque music so admired by Bunting, conducted by Boris Brott. Among the large audience were American poets Ed Dorn and Jonathan Williams.

The programme was as follows:

> *Albinoni Concerto a Cinque* in B flat with a series of short poems read by Bunting, e.g. from his collection *Loquitur*
>
> Vivaldi Flute Concerto in G minor
> (soloist David Haslam)
>
> Interval
>
> Vivaldi Bassoon Concerto in A minor
> (soloist Michael Chapman)
>
> Poems by Bunting: extracts from 'The Spoils' (2nd movement about Persia) and 'Brigg Flatts' (4th movement)
>
> *Corelli Concerto Grosso opus* 6 no. 1

A programme note by Tom Pickard read:

> 'Mr Bunting is primarily concerned with the music of a poem, and when composing will sometimes sacrifice meaning to produce a perfect sound. Hence his poetry is best communicated by the actual voice. Even when his meaning is sometimes too complex to absorb on first hearing, it is thrilling and moving in the musical arrangements of the words. This is his craft: delicacy, precision and care – and the result is often beautiful.'

A different sort of collaboration was the production of a folk opera, 'Cullercoats Tommy', involving Northern Stage, the Sinfonia, Folkworks and Dance City, as part of the Tall Ships Race celebrations of 1993. The story itself goes back to:

'New Year's Day, 1861. As a howling storm of blinding snow and sleet lashes the North East coast, the fisherwomen of Cullercoats drag the village lifeboat three miles overland to the rescue of the crew of The Lovely Nellie. All hands are saved, except for the young cabin boy Tommy Thompson.' (prog. note)

The work retells the story from several viewpoints: that of an artist who is painting a commemorative canvas of the scene; his children; the crew, who enact the tragedy as silent dancers; and through the eyes of the watchers and rescuers on the shore.

With libretto by Michael Wilcox and music by Edward McGuire, the work received six performances between 17 and 24 July 1993. The composer described his aim as follows:

'A modern, but widely understood musical language that can encompass the subtlety and depth of human emotions as well as be at one with the elemental power of nature is something I've been trying to develop in recent years. In "Cullercoats Tommy" I was fully confident to make the "broad brush strokes" necessary to create a true "people's opera". Since the early seventies I have advocated a revival of the power of tonality and melody in musical composition – a feeling stemming from deep political conviction as well as long involvement with traditional folk music.' (*ibid*.)

Folk song played an integral role in the composition, which was noted in *The Journal* as 'a fitting tribute to a brave young seaman.' (*Friends News* 1993)

## Not forgetting...

With so many concerts to their credit, there are bound to be some 'anomalies' – the odd occasion that is distinctly out of the ordinary (no embarrassment intended)...

'Some of the promotional exercises of that time were unreal, and one was hilarious. This was the occasion when the Orchestra was persuaded to play in a Gateshead quarry – but it rained on the day and the players had to retreat to a nearby hut, "saved from ignominy only by the weather", I wrote at the time.' (Tom Little, June 1963 *Prospectus* 1983–84 p. 40)

*'Cullercoats Tommy'*

*'Cullercoats Tommy'*

It was, as one player recalls, regarding the weather, an, 'unbelievably awful day': wet, hot and humid all at once. Nonetheless, the concert was given – but in the local village hall instead. Had things been otherwise, one wonders could this have been the start of a unique tour of North East and even national quarry venues?

Performances out of doors are always risky in this country – but underground? In 1964, some zealous miners are reported to have approached Boris Brott with a project for a concert in their coalmine – indeed they were busy hewing out an auditorium to get it all ready. 'Industrial' concerts, taking music to the workplace, have indeed been considered by Northern Sinfonia, but this particular gesture of cultural outreach was never to be realised, and Sir Humphrey Noble's barely polite denial of the report in the Press (in early April, please note) can only have added to the delight of the jokers behind it all. (Archive 5/1/15)

A novelty of a more seasonal sort was the Hoffnung Hogmanay concert in early January 1963. For this, members of Northern Sinfonia transformed into the Hoffnung Symphony Orchestra (leader Michael Jones), conducted by Malcolm Arnold and Lawrence Leonard, in association with the Hoffnung Oral Society and soloists including Annetta Hoffnung, to embark on the long-awaited Overture Leonora no. 4, Chagrin's 'Ballad of County Down' ('mostly in D major'), Matyas Seiber's setting of the 'The Famous Tay Whale' (text by the equally famous McGonagall), and a new 'Carnival of the Animals' by Arnold: Giraffe, Sheep, Cows ('A Coo's a Coo for a' That'), Mice, Jumbo, and the Bat ('on a ground row of 13 notes, sometimes transposed and when at rest in rows inverted.')(prog. in Archive 4/3/4)

There may be some disappointments, but also a good deal of humour in orchestral life!

**Concert series**

Beside the Connoisseur and Contact Concerts already mentioned, Northern Sinfonia had several new ideas for extra concert series, specifically designed to attract audiences in the North East.

A series of summer Promenade Concerts was begun in July 1962 and comprised five concerts, each sponsored by a local business firm. The fare was mainly 'light' in tone, including some Gilbert & Sullivan and a dramatic rendering of Tchaikovsky's 1812 Overture.

Concerning which, there is an interesting and cautionary tale, as told by General Manager Colin Ratcliffe when arranging to use the guns of the Royal Northumberland Fusiliers in the Tchaikovsky:

> 'We thought it would be rather fun (to use authentic guns)... but then the snags appeared. If they had been used inside the hall, every pane of glass might have been shattered – and half the audience frightened to death. So I tried to get permission from the city police to fire them in the street outside – but there is a by-law against that. We had to compromise all round. A gun will be placed in a backyard behind the City Hall, and a gunner will detonate a shot in the barrel, making a loud noise. How will he know when? I shall be standing near a door with a score watching the beat of the conductor, and at the right moment I will give the signal.' (*The Northern Echo*, Jul 1961)

Enterprising; but once a pattern of summer tours developed for Northern Sinfonia, the Prom initiative was not kept up, though several attempts to revive the idea have taken place. The matter of 'popular summer concerts in Newcastle' was debated in 1970, meeting with the objection that 'the summer is a bad time for the promotion of concerts in Newcastle.' (Finance Mins 28 Oct 1970) Nonetheless a 'Pensioners Prom' worked well in the 1981–82 season, and a Proms week was arranged in 1995 (7–14 October), comprising four evening concerts and a

'Last Night of the Proms'. (This 'Last Night' event is special to the fund-raising group North East Promenaders Against Cancer, set up by George Walker in 1990, in support of cancer research and cancer care centres in the North East.)

A more predictable season of the year is Christmastide, almost synonymous with 'concert'. While the theme is predetermined, there is still a wonderful range of music to draw on, for the Orchestra, for The Sinfonia Chorus, and of course the audience. A typical 'family' programme (as performed in 1976 at Middlesbrough Town Hall, Carlisle Market Hall Saturday and Newcastle City Hall, Sunday 17–19 December) consisted of classical music from the Orchestra in the first half, and communal carol singing in the second half. The Christmas concert could also be a more formal performance, such as Handel's 'Messiah'; or a purely secular affair, as in December 1980 when 'A Victorian Christmas Evening' was announced, with songs performed by Robert Tear and Benjamin Luxon. This featured some orchestral items and some involving The Sinfonia Chorus, and the evening ended with carols, 'led by The Full Company, conducted by Mr Alan Fearon, who Respectfully Invites the Participation of YOU the Ladies and Gentlemen of our Audience.' (prog. note)

An innovation, namely daytime concerts, was tried out in the mid-80s as the Van Walsum International Lunchtime Concerts – 'international' in recognition of the wide range of solo artists involved. These were designed to attract business people working in the city and older people who might not wish to travel to an evening concert; and though they ran at City Hall for two seasons 1984–86 and included such soloists as Igor Oistrakh, Marisa Robles, Kyung-Wha Chung, Nigel Kennedy and James Galway, it proved difficult to break even despite the sponsorship of English Estates. An analysis of the venture concluded,

> '... a lunchtime audience is essentially a casual one – nearly all tickets are sold on the door (rather than in advance) – neither the elderly (who presumably want to see what the weather is going to be like) nor those who are working and therefore have a limited lunch break, seem to wish to commit themselves in advance.' (Man. Mins 24 Apr 1986)

Nonetheless, the concept had considerable potential, as anyone who has witnessed the crowds that come into the centre of Newcastle on a busy shopping day will attest. The middle of the day is also convenient for older people who might not wish to travel during the darkness of a winter evening or those who have far to come (and go) on public transport, so the project was revived in 1995–96 with a set of concerts featuring the Brandenburg Concertos.

The choice of venue this time – the Brunswick Methodist Church – was inspired. It is centrally placed between Northumberland Street and the Monument, in the heart of Newcastle, but set back far enough from both these to be reasonably quiet. In itself, it is an impressive building, beautifully restored, its main space a delight of classical 1820 design with banks of wooden pews rising round the central space, giving an excellent view to all – and yet sufficiently compact to allow even small ensembles to be easily heard, in a pleasantly sociably sized auditorium. Not forgetting the convenient café on the ground floor.

In this new series of 'Lunchtime Concerts', though there have been some orchestral programmes, the emphasis was on ambitious chamber music, of a Classical mode. The 2003–04 season featured works by Beethoven, Schubert, Brahms, Handel, Vivaldi and Bach. An unmissable opportunity, 'to take a break from working or shopping for a rewarding hour or so of music...' (prog. note)

Another successful concept was to be 'Rush-hour Concerts', beginning at 5.45 pm – for those who would rather linger in the city after work (or shopping) than run the gauntlet of road or rail transport at that hour. Originally these were held at St Mary's Roman Catholic Cathedral (designed by no less a figure than Pugin), and

## The Late Mix 11/12/03

comprised a single chamber work like Mendelssohn's String Quintet in B flat or the Spohr Nonet. In 2002–03 the venue switched to St Andrew's Gallowgate (a gem of a church dating back to the twelfth century) with a programme built around the last eight symphonies of Mozart, directed by Bradley Creswick. At each performance actors were used to narrate a context for the works and read Mozart's letters from the relevant period. The lack of a raised platform and the problems of viewing that caused were overcome by the simple expedient of the orchestra playing standing up, with the cello section on risers. The audience at least could relax in those venerable surroundings and 'wind down at the end of the day.'

Bearing in mind the growing tendency to stay up late and enjoy the facilities Newcastle has to offer after dark, a series of late night concerts has been an attractive feature of recent Northern Sinfonia programming. Called 'The Late Mix' by virtue of its interesting range of music and musicians, the concerts were presented at All Saints, above the bustling Quayside, beginning at 9 pm.

This church is another of the marvels of Newcastle architecture, having a spectacular oval interior. Designed by David Stephenson in 1786, it has been hailed as, 'a totally successful adaptation of classical proportion and motif to the steepled church.' (Archive 5/1/25) Its exterior is a famous monument of the Tynescape; its interior with a capacity of around 600 is ideal for music-making. All Saints has a long relationship with the Orchestra having been the front runner in the 1980s for a new concert hall and administration space.

'A broad spectrum of music' was promised, in a performance 'augmented by lighting and staging managed by the Live Theatre.' In the 2003–04 season, the programmes centred on modern music – as befits the younger groups likely to be drawn to the area of an evening – including work by Bartók, John Casken, Shostakovich and James Macmillan (but also some Vivaldi, and a concert by the 'vocal big band' The SHOUT).

By utilising some of the fine architectural venues that Newcastle has to offer, and adapting the timing and content of the concerts to the audiences likely to attend, Northern Sinfonia (and its new management, North Music Trust) have provided welcome fare for many who might not venture to a traditional City Hall concert and given an extra dimension to the experience of music in Newcastle.

*All Saints, Newcastle, painting by W. Holmes*

## The Sinfonia Ensemble

A useful resource for broadening the repertoire and scaling performances to a variety of venues has been the concept of a Sinfonia Ensemble, begun in 1966. A debut concert was given in Newcastle in July of that year, followed by concerts in London and Manchester. The impetus came from the wind section: the group was guided by Enzo Muccetti, Director of the Parma Conservatory and tutor of Northern Sinfonia bassoonist, Michael Chapman; but the name soon came to imply a flexible selection of players from a range of the Orchestra's sections.

Defined rather prosaically as an, 'un-conducted group of less than 14 players,' the Ensemble concept has had a useful role to play in extending Northern Sinfonia's programme options – to make it 'more interesting, more lively, bring on more composers' – items by the Ensemble were soon included in Sinfonia concerts proper and in tours abroad in a pioneering development of programming practice.

Though the term 'Ensemble' is no longer used to distinguish sub-groups of the Orchestra, the concept remains valid – a logical consequence of the widely differing scale of concerts the Orchestra is called on to perform, and the natural ambition of players to explore and present the fuller repertoire of many centuries of writing for smaller as well as larger combinations of instruments. To this day, Northern Sinfonia benefits from introducing contrasts of scale into its concerts, as a valid resource of lively planning.

## Some opera

Opera is almost a separate tradition from orchestral/symphonic music, and considerably senior in its origin: some 150 years before the symphony became established, Monteverdi's 'L'Orfeo' of 1607 explored this new medium, intended paradoxically as a re-creation of ancient Greek and Roman drama. For some three centuries it remained the popular fashionable entertainment, indeed virtually the only multimedia activity of its kind until the arrival of cinema. Due to the large audiences it commanded, not a few composers found it profitable to devote themselves to opera almost exclusively, and the superb quality of the works of Mozart and Wagner (not forgetting Handel, Verdi, Tchaikovsky, Mussorgsky, Janáček and your own favourites) are highlights of Western music. As Rudolf Schwarz pointed out, 'if the Orchestra played no opera it would be denying itself 50 percent of the world's greatest music.' (Man. Mins 21 May 1969)

*The Sinfonia Ensemble*

In vain Northern Sinfonia management pointed out: 'In any foreign country, a city of the size, importance and wealth of Newcastle would be supporting at least one full symphony orchestra and an opera company as well.' (AGM 1961) Choral societies there are no lack of in the North; yet Northern Sinfonia's opportunities to play in opera were initially rather limited.

In 1961, General Manager Colin Ratcliffe suggested a series to be called 'Invitation to Opera' for the summer months. With the help of the distinguished basses, Owen Brannigan and David Franklin, a group of one-act comic operas was presented, including Gay's 'The Beggar's Opera', Bach's 'Coffee Cantata', Mozart's 'Bastien & Bastienne' and Haydn's 'The Apothecary'.

Northern Sinfonia was more often called upon to accompany the productions of local companies: Mozart's 'Magic Flute' was produced in the 1960–61 season with the Northumberland Teachers Opera Group; Stravinsky's 'Rake's Progress' in the 1963–64 season, in collaboration with Palatine Opera of Durham. Later, in 1970, they were engaged to play for a recording of Arne's short opera 'Thomas and Sally'; and more ambitiously a production of Purcell's 'Faery Queen' in 1973, in a form revised by Gareth Morgan and Keith Statham – a promotion in collaboration with the Tyneside Theatre Company. It presented a considerable editorial challenge, as Purcell's libretto was based on a bad adaptation of Shakespeare's 'A Midsummer Night's Dream'. Keith Statham explained: 'What Gareth Morgan and I decided to do was re-instate Shakespeare's verse (though with considerable cuts, and some linking material by John Barton), and insert most of Purcell's music where appropriate...' (prog. note). Alas, it did not prove a money-earner.

A major and much more profitable opportunity for Northern Sinfonia arose when Glyndebourne, the internationally renowned Sussex-based opera enterprise, decided to mount a touring company, parallel to its main

summer season at home. It not only gave understudies a chance to sing in main roles, but brought opera 'to major cities in the Midlands and North of England, whose distance from Glyndebourne prevented many people from attending performances there.' (*Stage & TV Today* 19 Oct 1967) From the first, Northern Sinfonia were engaged to provide the orchestra for these tours.

How this happened is explained by Tony Froud in the booklet *40 Years*:

> 'Glyndebourne had decided... it would now offer its quality to a wider audience by creating (with the help of Arts Council subsidy) the Glyndebourne Touring Opera. The LPO, which played for the Glyndebourne Festival, did not consider that it could, as a London Orchestra, commit itself to five consecutive weeks resident in five regional centres. The Touring Opera was therefore looking for an orchestra. Statham secured the contract for Northern Sinfonia. There were not a few mutterings about the indignity for Sinfonia musicians of playing in a pit, but the

resentments were of course not allowed to affect quality and Glyndebourne Touring Opera was launched in 1968 to critical acclaim with, at a time when opera reviews normally never wasted a word on the orchestra, special plaudits for Northern Sinfonia's contribution.'

The two conductors on these tours were provided by Glyndebourne; the orchestra in some cases had to be an augmented version of Northern Sinfonia. In 1968, the four operas proposed for the tour were 'Eugene Onegin', 'Fidelio', 'Entführung', and 'L' Incoronazione'. One Northern Sinfonia management committee member, David Roth (for the Orchestra) intervened to point out that, 'the first two listed of these four operas were not suitable for a chamber orchestra. He emphasised that he did not wish to object, but to ask the committee to be aware of the dangers of submerging the special identity of the NSO'. (Man. Mins 29 May 1968)

In fact, the experience for Sinfonia players was largely beneficial, and George MacDonald (clarinet) recalls that playing Mozart's Opera was a real help in understanding the composer's orchestral style – the 'vocal' line of the melodies, the 'dialogue' between instruments (and may we add – the sense of continual surprise and revelation?).

At a national level, the excellent reviews did much to boost Northern Sinfonia's image, and the additional income was especially welcome at a time of continuing financial uncertainty.

By September 1968, 'the whole committee agreed that it was certainly very much in the interests of the Orchestra that the Glyndebourne touring company should continue to thrive and the Orchestra should continue to be associated with it.' (Finance Mins)

The collaboration with Glyndebourne lasted till 1973; after which, regional duties and the opportunity to tour South America made for a full summer in 1974. Though it forms the most important episode in Northern Sinfonia's opera experience, there has been some excellent opera since – a good example would be the evening with Joan Sutherland singing extracts from operas by Verdi, Bellini, Donizetti and Auber at a Gala Concert at the Tyne Theatre in aid of the Prince's Trust (11 October 1989).

A memorable complete opera performance was that of 'Tosca' with Placido Domingo. Knowing him to be keen on football and the history of the theatre, Jack Dixon (manager of the Tyne Theatre in Westgate Road) arranged a prestige ticket for him to watch Newcastle Utd – and then persuaded him to sing in Puccini's 'Tosca' at the Tyne Theatre (with its fascinating historic stage machinery dating back to the 1860s). Mara Zampieri sang the title role in her debut in the UK. Though a one-off (6 May 1983), this is remembered by Northern Sinfonia players as a truly 'fantastic performance', and in the words of the Theatre's website, 'A Night of Sheer Magic.'

In another context, opera has come to feature significantly in Sinfonia recordings, with Britten's 'Albert Herring' (discussed under Recordings) and Vaughan Williams' 'Sir John in Love'.

A *Friends Newsletter* for December 2000 gives us an idea of the impact of the Vaughan Williams in performance:

> 'Audience members in the City Hall on the evening of 29 September [2000] will hopefully agree that orchestra and chorus, and the sixteen wonderful soloists, performing as a polished ensemble, produced a truly memorable concert. To be part of a performance of such a rarely staged work (which incidentally had taken two years to plan for and budget) may have been enough excitement but even more of a treat for chorus members is the opportunity to sing all those glorious English tunes again when we record the piece this month.'

The opera appeared as a two CD set from Chandos in 2001, a fitting tribute to Richard Hickox and, 'his passionate commitment to twentieth century English music.'

## The Sinfonia Chorus

'Singing is a basic human activity and a fundamental mode of cultural expression anywhere,' a report for Northern Sinfonia in 1988 justly points out. (Archive 2/8/2) The process by which a choir special to Northern Sinfonia has developed has been a relatively slow one, considering the appeal of choral performances for Northern audiences; The Sinfonia Chorus did not emerge until some 15 years after the founding of the orchestra itself.

Though Northern Sinfonia had collaborated with local choirs in performances prior to 1973, the advantages of having their own dedicated choir had long been apparent. Not only was there an appreciable audience demand for choral work, but such music was recognised to have contributed 'to the variety and quality of the repertoire throughout every period of musical history.' (Archive 2/8/2) The logical next step in developing the Orchestra was to establish a choir

> '... to permit the expansion of the Northern Sinfonia Orchestra's already wide repertoire by the addition of those works which it can perform when it has its own chamber chorus, trained to its own professional standards and in general under its own administration.' (*ibid*.)

*The Sinfonia Chorus conducted by Alan Fearon*

Keith Statham, as General Manager, raised the question of the need for a Sinfonia chorus in 1969, but at a time when the financial position of the Orchestra was not considered suitable by the Management Committee. The project was not lost sight of, however, and in 1972 a practical and economic way of setting an amateur choir up was devised: Alan Fearon would add to his existing duties of first-call timpanist and orchestral pianist those of chorus master, meaning that the choir could be inaugurated with, 'little extra expense other than the hire of rehearsal accommodation.'

It was settled that, 'advertisements would shortly be appearing announcing the formation of the choir and that auditions would begin in the second week of January 1973,' (Finance Mins 15 Nov 1972) leading to a summer of 'exacting rehearsals.'

In Alan Fearon's own words:

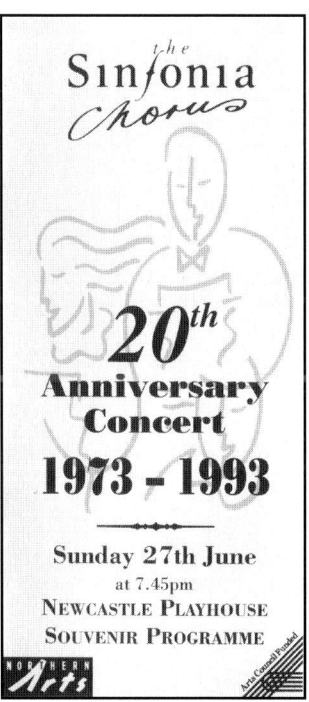

'... it was quite a shock when Keith Statham, the General Manager at the time, told me that the Board had agreed that a chamber choir should be formed and he wanted me to be the chorus master! When I pointed out to him that this was a bit of a risk considering my limited experience he reassured me by saying, "Don't worry, if you are no good we will kick you out!"

When we advertised the auditions we had an amazing response, with 200 people applying from which we chose 40. Then I had to find a rehearsal day which suited everyone so we sent out questionnaires and to my horror 30 out of 40 chose Sunday, so Sunday it had to be. As this was long before The Sinfonia Centre was built, our rehearsals were held in the Clayton Road Methodist Church Hall... and it was a memorable moment when we all met there for the first time and sung through some difficult unaccompanied pieces by Moeran. There was no time to waste as we had to prepare for an *a capella* concert in Stockton followed by a BBC recording in King's Hall and, finally, the most nerve-racking moment of all, the first concert with the orchestra, conducted by Christopher Seaman, which began with Handel's "Zadok the Priest" and finished with Haydn's "Nelson Mass". I remember how puzzled people were when they saw so few singers walking on to the stage and how surprised they were when after that wonderful tension-building introduction, The Sinfonia Chorus burst out with the opening words of "Zadok the Priest". I had managed to survive the first test...'
(*40 Years*)

Statham's offer was not entirely a chance act: he knew Alan as a player with Northern Sinfonia since 1968 and was aware of his work as repetiteur and singing coach with the Palatine Opera Group in Durham. His trust was well placed, as can be seen by the reviews of that first concert with Northern Sinfonia, November 1973 at Middlesbrough Town Hall:

'Peter Haigh wrote in the *Cleveland Evening Gazette* "Let it be said straight away that this choir, newly formed though it is, shows in full measure all the best features of the North's Great Choral tradition."

John Healy informed readers of *The Journal* that, "The newly formed Sinfonia Chorus made its debut in Newcastle City Hall last night in a magnificent performance of Haydn's 'Nelson' Mass."

In *The Guardian* Gerald Larner wrote that, "the Chorus proved itself capable of producing a wide variety of colour and sustaining a firm ensemble... it is obviously a promising chorus which will be an asset to the Northern Sinfonia.'" (Archive 2/8/2)

Before The Sinfonia Chorus had completed one full season of activity, Tom Little was already writing in *The Northern Echo* that it was 'a superbly disciplined and highly musical group which produces beautiful, homogeneous choral tone... Mr Fearon clearly has flair as a choral conductor.' (prog. 15 Dec 1983)

Northern Sinfonia itself was equally impressed by the results. As Tony Froud recalls:

> 'The first time that Rudolf Schwarz conducted the Chorus (in unaccompanied Brahms motets, as I remember, but within an orchestral concert) he commented that it was, "the finest choral instrument that I have conducted since the BBC Singers." And remember, that's not the BBC Chorus, but the professional (chamber) choir.' (Archive 7/9)

The Sinfonia Chorus was soon much in demand:

> 'In the first season of its existence Alan Fearon's Sinfonia Chorus made a Christmas television programme for Tyne Tees Television and recorded a BBC broadcast, apart from its work with the Northern Sinfonia Orchestra and for regional music societies. Since then, these three branches of its activities have made enormous demands upon the spare time of its dedicated amateur members. A typical week for them when they are performing with the Orchestra will run, for instance: Sunday, regular rehearsal; Tuesday, concert rehearsal; Wednesday, Thursday, Friday, performances; Sunday, regular rehearsal again.' (Archive 2/8/2)

The dedication of members is stressed in notes on a carol concert recorded for Tyne Tees Television on 13 December 1973:

> 'The Sinfonia Chorus is entirely amateur, but such is the devotion of its members that in a week like the present one they perform their full-time jobs and then give up five evenings to making music with the Sinfonia!'

Amateurs they may be, but as regards commitment and performance, the same professional ethos applies to them as to Northern Sinfonia – a point taken up in programme notes of 27 June 1993:

> 'Members of the Chorus are from all walks of life, including business people, doctors, engineers, housewives/husbands, lawyers and teachers and are all amateurs committed to the standards expected when singing with an internationally renowned professional orchestra.'

On the international front, the Chorus has taken part in two trips abroad. In 1980, they joined Northern Sinfonia in concerts during Holy Week in Spain, with Jean-Bernard Pommier conducting. There were concerts in a theatre in Burgos as well as churches in Madrid and the beautiful city of Cuenca. The Madrid concert is vividly recalled by a Chorus member as, 'performing Haydn's 'Creation' with Jean-Bernard Pommier whilst precariously perched on pews in a Madrid church packed to bursting point.' (Archive 2/8/2) In 2000, they attended the Festival at Suilly-sur-Loire, also with Pommier, performing the Beethoven Choral Fantasia and Mozart's C minor Mass.

The Chorus now has a fine list of recordings to its credit, including the Bliss 'Pastorale', Vaughan Williams' 'Sir John in Love', a fine rendering of the noble finale to Beethoven's 9th Symphony, and the exquisite Mozart Requiem:

'The most recent (1989) Sinfonia recording including the Chorus to be released is the Mozart Requiem. Again recorded in All Saints Church on the Quayside, sponsored by Tyne and Wear Development Corporation, it is conducted by Richard Hickox and features a star line-up of soloists. It reached the record shops in time for the climax of the commemoration of the bicentenary of Mozart's death, and exemplifies what The Sinfonia Chorus is all about. It is a recording for a major record label of mainstream repertoire (repertoire which is only available to the Orchestra because the Chorus exists). It was "put in the can" during four intense recording sessions that devoured an entire weekend during a bitterly cold spell in January which would try the commitment of the most avid amateur musician. Yet such is its quality that it enters a potentially overcrowded market for Mozart Requiems with all the potential of competing – on the same terms — with the best of them.' (Archive 2/8/2)

The 2003–04 season marked The Sinfonia Chorus' 30th year and three special and challenging concerts were arranged, representative of the scale and scope of their repertoire over the span of 30 years. The first of these included 'Songs of Springtime' by Moeran, a piece that featured in their very first *a capella* concert back in 1973. The second concert was Handel's 'Alexander's Feast', conducted by Nicholas McGegan – a new work for the Chorus but one that aptly represents the long-standing respect for oratorio in the North. The finale of the three, recalling the larger-scale projects the Chorus has tackled in the past, was a performance of Bach's St Matthew Passion with Northern Sinfonia conducted by Sir Roger Norrington. A fitting setting for this concert was provided by the Cathedral of St Nicholas in Newcastle, with choir and instrumentalists at the crossing, and the audience packing the nave and aisles.

An important role is assured for the Chorus as part of The Sage Gateshead in the twenty-first century:

'Choral singing of every shape and size will be a vital part of the work that goes on in The Sage Gateshead and the Chorus will be at the centre of that work.' (NS *Music* Feb–Apr 2004)

In an encouraging new development, a youth choir is also envisaged, 'a choral equivalent of the Young Sinfonia'. We all wish these ventures well, and look forward to the projects Simon Halsey, as their new conductor, will be undertaking with the Chorus in 2005.

## Film music

An unusual concert opportunity arose when Chris Yates (General Manager) was approached by Sheila Whittaker, who ran the Tyneside Cinema, to provide orchestral accompaniment for a showing of the silent film 'Napoleon' at the Tyneside Film Festival in 1981. Alan Fearon, in view of his experience conducting the Chorus (or because, 'I often do weird and wonderful things') was invited to conduct Carl Davis' score at a live performance. When the score arrived in the post – in many huge volumes – the scale of the work began to be apparent! The veteran French film-maker Abel Gance made several versions of Napoleon's life for the screen, initially in 1927, and it was this early version, reconstructed by Alan Brownlow, and slightly shortened to five hours, that Carl Davis wrote a new score for, drawing on appropriate music like Beethoven's 'Eroica'. (Five hours? Fortunately the film is renowned for its action sequences and mobile camera shots.) Essential rehearsal for Alan was to mime conducting to a video of the film, to get a sense of the pace, and some experience in the exacting co-ordination of sound and image such work requires. The orchestra for the real event was of course Northern Sinfonia, and we hear that the performance, put on as almost a series of films over a day, was received with tremendous applause – leading to further opportunities including a screening in Holland with Alan conducting the Brabant Orchestra.

This success was followed up by Alan Fearon conducting Shostakovich's score for the film 'New Babylon' in 1982. This is a tale of a romance, unpromisingly between a Parisian shop-girl and a Prussian soldier in 1871 against the background of the Franco-Prussian War. The film was made in 1929 with directors Grigory Kozintsev and Leonid Trauberg. The musical score, Shostakovich said, was shaped, 'to coincide with the motion picture's tempo and rhythm and increase its effect.' Critics have not been kind about the 'suite' extracted from the film score – it is seldom appropriate to play such music in isolation – but this only reinforces the value of having authentic performances of early films with live music.

In 1983, a third silent film was screened, this time 'An Italian Straw Hat' with a score specially commissioned from Benedict Mason (using some of Ibert's original incidental music for the stage version). The film is a 'screwball comedy': a bridegroom on the way to church is delayed when his horse nibbles a lady's straw hat en route – her sweetheart demands an immediate replacement for the hat... and so on. The film version was directed by René Clair in 1927, and proved a challenge to Alan Fearon and Northern Sinfonia in terms of the split-second timing that comic action (and its musical counterpart) depends on for its effect.

After Alan had performed 'Napoleon' in Holland with the Brabant Orchestra, they requested he tackle the score by Edmund Meisel for Eisenstein's great film 'Battleship Potemkin'. This proved quite a task as comparison of the orchestral parts with the piano score indicated that several instrumental parts had been lost. Alan set about reconstructing these with the help of Northern Sinfonia trumpet player Roger Payne. Meisel (1874–1930) was Austrian by birth, and collaborated with Eisenstein on the film score for the première in Berlin in 1926. It is said that Eisenstein did not want 'tone painting' from Meisel but insisted that the music, 'should be rhythm, rhythm, and before all else rhythm.' (Which may account

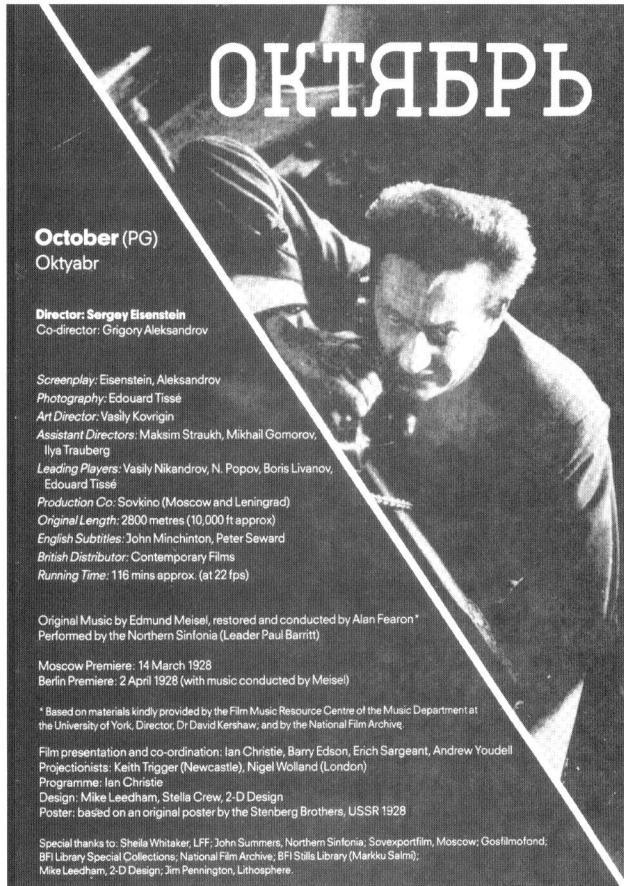

for the large use Meisel makes of the percussion section.)

A second Meisel/Eisenstein collaboration was to take place in 1988 when Alan Fearon

> '... reconstructed Meisel's score to Eisenstein's other epic masterpiece "October", which he has since performed with Northern Sinfonia in Newcastle, Cambridge, the London Film Festival, the Avignon Festival, Paris, Grenoble and Le Havre.' (prog. note)

Again, the score proved problematic. A very large orchestra was called for, including trombones and much percussion, but the piano score showed that the surviving orchestral parts were incomplete. When Alan and Roger had restored these, another surprise was in store, for when the score was checked against a video of the film, the action didn't always fit the 'cues' in the piano score, suggesting there was more than one version of the film in existence. This was unexpected, and led to a Tyne Tees Television programme 'The Meisel Mystery', a documentary on the discoveries made during the reconstruction of the score. In the event, a modified score fitting the available film version was produced and performed with great success.

## Festivals

One curious historical aspect of programming is the concept of the 'season' which goes back to the time when the landed gentry would be busy on their estates during the summer, but free to migrate to town in the winter to seek entertainment. (The 'season' for Northern Sinfonia begins conceptually on 1 October each year – even today the modern urbanite has other recreations to fill the summer evenings.) Once Northern Sinfonia musicians were retained on permanent contract, there have been two main solutions for the out-of-season period – music festivals and tours.

Newcastle at one time had its own late summer festival of the arts. After a brave showing in 1969, the 1970 Festival expanded to comprise some 300 events in 15 days.

> 'The programme embraces drama, art exhibitions, film seasons, late night entertainment, large symphony concerts, lunch-time Beethoven recitals, pop concerts, folk evenings, late night chamber music, ceilidhs and morning lectures by well-known writers…' (*Prospectus* 1970–71 p. 24)

An early contribution by Northern Sinfonia was a work called 'The Lambton Worm', commissioned from David Barlow and narrated by Alex Glasgow, in 1969. Despite a financial loss on the 1971 festival, the series continued and in 1978 included classical music, light music, exhibitions, cinema, theatre, rock and jazz, folk, a food festival, talks and lectures (William Burroughs, Sid Chaplin, and Tom Haddaway), a Lord Mayor's Procession, a Sanskritic Festival, fashion shows, and much more. It was also the context for some notable performances by Northern Sinfonia accompanying silent films. On another occasion, a Sinfonia Ensemble risked playing a rather challenging piece by Villa-Lobos at a concert at the Laing Art Gallery, to find themselves recorded by the BBC and broadcast several times as one of the highlights of the festival.

The North East has also seen music festivals at Hexham, Durham and Ashington. Of a concert that took advantage of the splendid historic venues available in the city, *The Durham County Advertiser* wrote:

> 'The setting fitted the mood, the occasion and the music. In the Great Hall of Durham Castle, Northern Sinfonia Orchestra opened the 1966 Durham Music Festival on Sunday evening, playing under two conductors and before an audience which filled the hall and enjoyed the delightful music.' (11 Nov 1966)

Music festivals are a popular format across the country, and have provided excellent experience and good publicity for Northern Sinfonia over the years. As the NEAA pointed out, 'A festival is an excellent way of focusing attention on the arts.' (NEAA Annual Report 1964–65) A sample of Northern Sinfonia's engagements would include the festivals at Aberdeen, Aldeburgh (founded by Benjamin Britten, and with a splendid acoustic in the converted maltings), Bath (in 1968, when it was still a 'close-knit small festival atmosphere' and again in 2003 by when it had transformed into a much larger scale event), Cheltenham (where modern music was favoured), Edinburgh, Leeds, Lichfield, Llandaff (where Northern Sinfonia premièred William Matthias' Horn Concerto in 1984), Spalding, Swansea, 'The Three Spires' (at Truro Cathedral, directed by Richard Hickox, and coyly echoing the much older 'Three Choirs' Festival of Gloucester/Hereford/Worcester) – to name but a few!

Music festivals abroad were another source of opportunity for Northern Sinfonia. The first such tour occurred almost by chance, when at the last moment the Stuttgart Chamber Orchestra was unable to play at the 1963 Menton Festival. Apparently Eugene Istomin (who had played with Northern Sinfonia) secured an invitation for the Orchestra, which Sir Humphrey Noble, aware of the advantages of such an opportunity, was happy to endorse. Thus it was the Orchestra set off (by coach) to play at Menton.

The concerts were staged out of doors – in the little square before the town's Baroque church – rehearsals were held

> '... in front of the church at 10.30 in the morning but it was still hot; and this, together with the out of door acoustics, made work difficult even without the unfailing interruptions: howling babies, a pair of rival clocks striking eleven and noon, and occasional insolent intruders...' (Antony Cullen in NS prog. 27 Sep 1963)

Fortunately, concerts proper were held in the gentle warmth of the evening. They were conducted by American Milton Katims; Isaac Stern was the violin soloist. A promising beginning, and one that found them already hailed as, 'the region's ambassadors of good music.' (*The Journal* 2 Aug 1963)

One of the most prestigious of these events is the Festival at Prades in southern France. It came about in 1950 because Pablo Casals was unwilling to travel to the US to play. The response of Alexander Schneider was:

> 'You cannot condemn your art to silence. Since you do not wish to leave Prades, will you allow us – a group of musicians – to come to you and give some concerts with you?' (1975 Fest. prog. in translation)

Northern Sinfonia first played there in 1975 under Jean-Bernard Pommier in the Abbey Church of Saint Michel de Cuxa, and were sure of a warm welcome thereafter:

> 'The concert of 8 August has allowed us to hear once more the Northern Sinfonia of England, who were at Prades before in 1975 and 1985. This year the festival is under the direction of Wilfried Boettcher, who attended it when Casals was alive, and so the tradition

The Sinfonia Chorus rehearsing in Spain (1963)

of Prades is both continued and revitalised...' (Archive 2/6/26–27, in translation)

Many such opportunities to play in festivals abroad have featured in the Orchestra's calendar, serving as an encouragement for Northern Sinfonia to travel yet further afield...

## Tours

Not many people are likely to think of joining an orchestra in order to see the world, but members of Northern Sinfonia have certainly been involved in some amazing trips abroad, as well as many tours of duty in the UK.

Tours abroad are much to do with 'international visibility'. Practically speaking, 'Overseas work is obtained either when the Orchestra is invited to tour or when a project specially designed is sold to an overseas agent or promoter.' (NS Corp. Plan 1988–91) The costs are inevitably high, and generally a tour can only be considered if sponsorship is forthcoming and a chain of concerts can be arranged to make the travel worthwhile.

Northern Sinfonia's first large-scale project was ambitious enough – a major tour of Canada and the USA in 1967, set up by Boris Brott to coincide with the Expo '67 in Montreal. It was considered musically most rewarding – but the combination of travel costs and lack of hoped-for sponsorship made it a significant burden on the Orchestra's finances.

*Off to the New World (1967)*

*George Malcolm*

The situation improved with a series of tours of Germany from 1970 on, made possible when George Malcolm told his German agent that his choice was to have Northern Sinfonia accompany him. The tour in January 1970 visited West Germany and Switzerland, offering a choice of works by Bach, Dvořák, Handel, Haydn, Mozart, Schubert and Stamitz.

The tour of 1974 included Malcolm as harpsichordist/conductor and Barry Tuckwell on horn, and comprised 11 concerts in Germany plus two in Holland (for which Yoav Talmi conducted). The programme for the tour had been perfected in concerts at home and consisted of Haydn Symphony no. 77 in B flat, Copland 'Quiet City', Mozart Horn Concerto in E flat K447, Krommer Partita in F for Wind Instruments op. 57, plus either the Frank Martin Concerto for Harpsichord and Small Orchestra or Haydn Harpsichord Concerto in D, and finally the Bach Brandenburg Concerto no. 2 in F.

The success of this tour can be judged by the reviews:

> 'The Sinfonia... combines all the virtues of a permanent chamber orchestra, such as a varied, flexible dynamic range and extreme precision of balance between the sections.' (*Kölnische Rundschau*)

> 'Whilst the programme as a whole could be seen as a gradual ascent towards perfection, the performance of Bach's second Brandenburg Concerto was undoubtedly the summit. David Haslam (flute), Helen Powell (one of the best lady oboists we have been lucky enough to hear), Barry Wilde (violin), Barry Tuckwell and George Malcolm, together with the orchestra, presented us with a model performance...' (*Main-Echo*)

> Through the art of Barry Tuckwell, Mozart's Horn Concerto, K.447, became a delicacy of the first order... The ensemble, led by the soloist and excellent leader, Barry Wilde, was first-class... In the Frank Martin concerto we were fascinated, as always, by George Malcolm's artistic personality and virtuosity... the conductorless orchestra played with impressive precision.' (*Volksblatt*, Stuttgart)

> 'The secret of the Sinfonia... lies in its ability to combine chamber-music sensitivity and lightness of touch with the splendid, fuller sound of a large orchestra' (*Hannoversche Presse*)

> 'For two hours... the public held their breath for fear of disturbing the fine web of sound.' (*Stuttgarter Nachrichten*)

In retrospect, players single out the marvellous performances of the Frank Martin Harpsichord Concerto – though broadcast on radio at the time by Hesse Rundfunk, a copy cannot now be traced.

With a tour of East Europe and Italy in 1971, Germany in 1972, Holland in 1973 (where Northern Sinfonia played in two of the finest concert halls in Europe – the Concertgebouw Hall in Amsterdam and the De Doelen Hall in Rotterdam), a tour of Scandinavia 'culminating in the magnificent new Konserthus in Oslo, where we were the first visiting orchestra to play,' (*Prospectus* 1983–84, p. 31) and a tour of South America in 1974, it is clear that Northern Sinfonia had launched itself on an ambitious international programme.

*The Musikverein, Vienna (1978)*

In 1978, the Northern Sinfonia began a European tour that brought them to perhaps the most famous concert hall of all:

> 'Now for the highlight of the tour – Vienna. Having travelled all night in a train from Hanover, we arrived in Wien at 3 o'clock in the afternoon. The weather was milder than the bitter winds of Kiel. Next to the hotel, people were swimming in the open air in hot springs.
>
> The Musikverein is steeped in musical tradition and you can't help feeling that Brahms and Schubert are listening in the wings. Everyone suffered a bit from nerves except Barry Tuckwell who played Mozart's 4th Horn Concerto beautifully. He joined us here for the next leg of the tour...' (Martin Shillito [NS horn player] in *Friends News* Jun 1978)

However, the prestige was not only for Northern Sinfonia; in some sense they were acting as international cultural ambassadors – as John Summers put it, 'It's crucial for the region of Newcastle upon Tyne to be able to point to something home-grown which is competing successfully on an international level.' (Archive 3/3/32) There was a decided element of national promotion, and in return for British Council support of such tours it was customary to include British compositions in the programmes abroad. Thus for the 1971 tour of Eastern Europe and Italy, four concerts were offered to promoters, each containing one English work by Britten, Bliss or Arnold.

British Council support was particularly important in financing and managing the major tour of South America in 1974. Clarinetist Graham Evans provided the following summary:

> '... the Northern Sinfonia Orchestra visited Brazil, Argentina, Chile, Peru, Nicaragua, Mexico, Jamaica and Trinidad in a tour lasting six weeks. Thirty players with guest conductor Norman del Mar and soloists Sandra Browne and Manoug Parikian gave 19

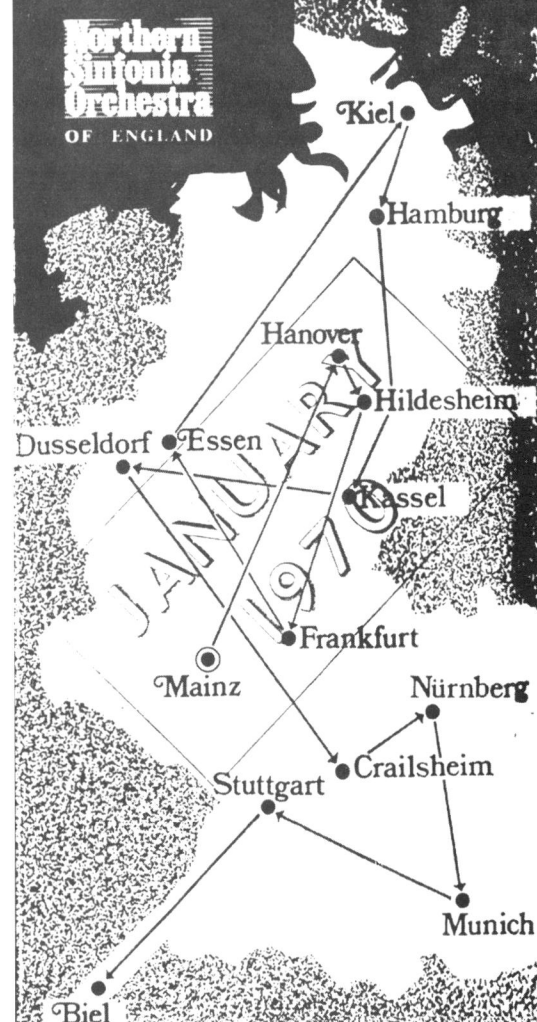

concerts, travelling over 25,000 miles with 27 air take-offs and landings, and stops in 13 different hotels.

The Orchestra played five different programmes, including symphonies by Haydn, Mozart and Schubert, with twentieth century music by Bartók, Seiber and Stravinsky... English music was represented by works by Berkeley, Britten and Walton, and South American composers also featured in our programme: a bassoon concerto by Villa-Lobos and a flute quintet by Ginastera.' (Archive 5/1/30)

Something of the delights and stresses and sheer pell-mell activity of this tour can be gleaned from rough notes that survive in the archive (2/6/67); here, a glimpse of the opening acclimatisation leading to first concerts:

**'Sunday July 14**

    7.00 am – Arrive Airport Rio (11 am GMT)

    9.20 am – Hotel – Money

    10.00 am – Café, beer

    12.30 pm – Lunch, Taverna

    12.45–2.00 pm – Shishkebab £1

    2.00 pm – Coach to Sugarloaf, two cable cars, fantastic view, lots of people... Japanese coach to [statue of] Christ – stairs – miss bus – fares chaos – hotel

    7.00 pm – Beers

    7.45 pm – Taxi to party

    8.15–12.00 pm – Collapse

**Monday July 15**

    10.15 am – Breakfast, paw-paw and mango balls, banana, cheese, coffee...

    1.00 pm – Walk about

    2.00 – 5.00 pm – Rehearse – Theatre men building scenery on stage

    6.00 pm – Meal – salted codfish, grilled and boiled potatoes, local speciality...

    9.00 –11.00 pm – Concert'

Another day, another concert:

> 'São Paolo. A teeming ant-hill. Cars. People. Thousands of high-rise flats. Incredible. I've never seen anything like it. Far bigger and noisier than London, must be a bit like Osaka... Hotel good. Lovely single room. Beautiful theatre. People to go to a Samba club after concert. Didn't. Too tired...'

Hectic, certainly, and fun, probably, but consider also the reflections of Noel Broome, after the tour of Germany in 1970, which involved concerts at Hanover, Hildesheim, Kiel Castle, Hamburg, Kassel, Crailsheim, Nuremberg, Munich, Stuttgart, and Biel.

> 'Foreign tours have a special place in an orchestra's career: the most important motive behind them is prestige. Despairing of vociferous and overwhelming support on its home-ground, many an orchestra has to earn its laurels in the capital and abroad... and however much we family men may groan at yet another stretch in foreign parts, with all that it implies: suitcase existence, communal life with colleagues and hours of morale-breaking travel, we have to admit to the need for these periodic excursions.' (*Prospectus* 1970–71 p. 30)

Perhaps the answer is to balance travelling and playing with relaxation, not forgetting the need to cover all eventualities. On an expedition to Bobigny near Paris in 1989 the, 'miscellaneous personal items in van' included one sewing machine, four sets of golf clubs, one gents bicycle, and one holdall containing bassoon reed-making tools. (Archive 2/7/9)

There is a limit after all to the amount of (often rather expensive) sight-seeing that can be fitted in between performances. (In this case the tremendous productions of Mozart directed by American, Peter Sellars.)

There were further tours of the New World to mark Northern Sinfonia's silver jubilee year in 1984, and again in February, 1988 when

> 'There had been a lot of missionary work and... several prime dates. The audience in Carnegie Hall for Northern Sinfonia had apparently been bigger than for many major symphony orchestras which had played there recently.'

Ron Thorndycraft's report continues,

> '… [he] had been impressed that 13 of the 14 promoters had chosen programmes including contemporary English music (although the tastes of their audiences were evidently not so wide), and with the high level of hall equipment even in small places.' (Man. Mins 2 Mar 1988)

His only reservation was the agency should have arranged 'concerts in the coldest part of America at the coldest time of the year.' Oboist Colin Kellett noted temperatures of -60 degrees in Grand Forks, Dakota: 'The coach had to keep its engine running all night long to prevent the diesel from freezing.' (*Friends News* Mar 1999)

It was just as well the Orchestra had been seriously warned, before setting off:

> 'Do not forget that the weather will be quite unlike any experienced in the UK. As well as suitable clothing it may be advisable to take dark glasses because of the very bright light in places where there is snow on the ground.' (Archive 2/6/31–32)

A pleasant contrast are Noel Broome's reflections on Hungary in the May of 1979:

> 'By the shores of Lake Balaton we sat down and drank, not only the wine, but also the sunshine, with what even our sternest critics would have agreed was a triumphant concert behind us in Budapest, where, by some mysterious alchemy, everything – acoustics, audience and morale – had conspired to make this the musical high point of the tour. There remained the final concert, in Vezprem, of academic interest only had it not been for the uncanny ability of Tamás Vásáry, soloist in Mozart's B flat Concerto, K.595, to turn a piano with no guts into the finest of Steinways, and that in a theatre with the dryest of cardboard acoustics. Our hotel overlooking the lake had every Western comfort, the staff were friendly and helpful, and home was in sight; by now we were past worrying whether George [Malcolm] would remember to give us that crucial up-beat in the Frank Bridge, and was it in Bratislava or Debrecen that a viola-player dropped his bow in Brandenburg 3?...' (*Prospectus* 1979–80)

A fine array of prestigious engagements has followed over the years. In 1992, there was a trip to Japan: a Northern Sinfonia concert in Tokyo was attended by Crown Prince Naruhito. In November 1999, Northern Sinfonia were called on to perform at the opening of The National Centre for the Performing Arts in Bombay (Mumbai) in India – en route to Germany!

How does everyone cope with the multiplicity of languages encountered? Fortunately, music is a universal tongue, welcomed everywhere, but even so it must have been reassuring to find Norwegian newspapers reviewing a concert in 1977 as 'Suksess for Northern Sinfonia' and 'Sinfonia Triunf!'

## The virtual concert

A concert without an audience – or without a visible audience, reacting and contributing – is one way to think of broadcasting and recording. There are gradations of remoteness – a 'direct relay' from a public concert via radio or television retains much of the atmosphere of the real event, as would a 'deferred relay' – the same material broadcast at a later date. A studio recording of concert pieces for future broadcast might gain in sound quality but lack audience reaction. Technically most demanding is recording for issue on gramophone record, cassette or CD. Not quite the same as being there in person but there is no doubt the improved ways of sharing music made possible by ever-new technologies have had a major impact on the Orchestra's operation, and recording sessions have been an important part of the modern musician's working life, especially since the advent of LPs in the late 1950s.

Recording and broadcasting, it was recognised, 'represent enormously valuable opportunities to enhance the reputation of the Orchestra and expand its audience outside the region.' (Corp. Plan 1988–89) For Northern Sinfonia, such broadcasts could be profitable options they were not slow to see the advantage of. In May 1959, the Orchestra was first broadcast on radio. There soon followed a contract to play for the Tyne Tees Television programme 'Your Kind of Music', a monthly commitment, which fitted in well with the nascent Orchestra's schedule: it took up two days at the TV studios (though as a live show, the final filming could be 'quite nerve-wracking'). It required a considerable commitment of time and effort on both sides, but one that could be justified in terms of the television company's policy of devoting a proportion of airtime to cultural enterprises. As Tyne Tees Television were able to pay players a fee plus expenses, these engagements were important in encouraging high-quality musicians to travel to Newcastle, to the benefit of Northern Sinfonia's main concert series.

What would they be playing? Tyne Tees Television's Programme Controller, Bill Lyon-Shaw described 'Your Kind of Music' as 'not a highbrow programme, but a serious attempt to present good music in an entertaining and colourful way. It will not be confined to the so-called classics; it will include good music of all kinds.' (Archive 5/1/2)

As programme contents show, the range of music was not that which we usually associate with Northern Sinfonia, but it was a matter for some congratulation when a second series of the show was broadcast in 1961. The continuation of this programme was symbolic of the excellent relations between Northern Sinfonia and Tyne Tees Television, exemplified when Anthony Jelly of Tyne Tees became Chairman of Northern Sinfonia in 1969.

A different series, 'The Magic of Music', was pre-recorded for Tyne Tees Television in 1965, with Northern Sinfonia conducted by Rudi Schwarz and Boris Brott. It comprised 13 programmes, 18 minutes long, one of which featured the Orchestra's leader, Joseph Segal, playing the last movement of Mozart's Violin Concerto in A.

A mirror series, though with a more educational slant, was called 'The Making of Music'. Presented by Boris Brott, the 13 programmes of 25 minutes each were broadcast starting November 1967. This series was concerned with 'talking about how and why we make music,' and included Northern Sinfonia players in 10 episodes, also jazzman Danny Moss, Gerry Marsden of the Pacemakers, Wilfred Josephs, a brass band and others.

Producer/Director Richard Doubelday said:

> 'Our aim is to show people how much they already know about music, without perhaps realising it and to try very gently and entertainingly to broaden that

knowledge so that they enjoy music even more.'
(*The Viewer* 11–17 Nov 1967)

An impressive set was devised with a super-sized orchestral score as the studio floor: players stood on their own line of music to play!

In addition, there have been a number of films for TV made about Northern Sinfonia. The BBC documentary, 'A Chamber Orchestra in Newcastle? You must be mad', in their series *Workshop*, from 1966, was a compilation of interviews with Sinfonia players and (notably) conductor Boris Brott; lasting an hour, it climaxes with a performance of the first movement of Mozart's Symphony no. 29. A copy of this has been recently deposited with the Northern Sinfonia archive. A second film by Tyne Tees Television, 'Behind the bow-ties', has been reported, but we have yet to locate a copy; also a possible recording of Eisenstein's 'Oktober' with the reconstructed score in place. Information welcome!

Last but not least, there have been the radio broadcasts recorded in studio conditions for later use. These would be made with the BBC; fortunately a good number of these recordings have survived on tape and are housed in the National Sound Archive. Radio broadcasts (direct and deferred) proved a dependable item in Northern Sinfonia's schedule, averaging 6–7 a year throughout the 1990s, and remain one of the most realistic ways of sharing music outside the concert hall.

## Recordings

'In the general view of the profession, recordings are the best possible publicity for any orchestra,' said Northern Sinfonia minutes (24 Jun 1987).

A good recording, coupled with a good review, certainly helps promote an orchestra, both in the public consciousness and in terms of attracting concert work, here and abroad.

This led to a recording being seen as something of a privilege, with relatively little financial benefit for the Orchestra. In 1970:

'Mr Statham reported that the Orchestra was to undertake 12 sessions to make three LPs for EMI, to be released late this year and during the first quarter of next year on the full-price HMV label... he regarded it as vital that the Orchestra should appear on a major international record label.' (Finance Mins 9 Jun)

He put the case strongly, because he also had to announce that the recordings were to be made for free 'this time' (though EMI would cover the cost of extra players). In general, a recording would be made without any advance; the fees of players would be paid by the record company, and later on, royalties paid to conductor and soloists.

The recording process was always scheduled to take several sessions, including a final play-through of the complete piece. This enabled an optimum master to be constructed by skilled editing of the tapes. (Unlike a live concert, where some uncertainties were admissible, a published version, designed to be listened to repeatedly, needs to be free of flaws.) After that, there might be a wait of a year or so before the recording was issued, though in the case of the Handel Coronation Anthems – made for the Queen's Silver Jubilee year – the LPs were pressed and out in the shops in three weeks!

Another convention of the record trade is to reissue titles, sometimes under a different label in a different medium, or to use a part of a recording in a new compilation, as has happened with individual pieces by Bliss and Britten in Northern Sinfonia's case. It makes preparing a discography difficult, but perhaps in due course, we will see some of Northern Sinfonia's work reappear as select 'historic' recordings.

The very first Sinfonia recordings were set up and conducted by Boris Brott, in 1966, using the Old Banqueting Hall in Jesmond Dene and Ravenshill Social

Club as recording venues. The company issuing them was Mace of New York (a subsidiary of Sceptre Records) – this turned out to be two keen Americans bearing their own recording gear. The choice of a club in Gateshead as venue proved less than ideal: it was set back from the road alright, but unexpected background noise came from the club itself in the form of subliminal boom from a necessarily much-used door.

Copies of these early recordings (never formally released in this country) were recently deposited in the archive by Boris Brott, and it has been interesting to listen to the spirited string playing of Northern Sinfonia from so long ago. The set of Handel opera suites, the 'Petite Symphonie for Wind' by Gounod, and Britten's 'Simple Symphony' are particularly attractive; and there are occasional solo passages by the Sinfonia's leader, Joseph Segal, to be savoured.

The number of recordings increased considerably when Richard Hickox was with the Northern Sinfonia, notably in the field of English and choral music. Some prestige recordings were made with EMI/HMV, and a long-term relationship established with the Academy Sound and Vision (ASV) label. Academy Sound and Vision was a London-based company, set up when Decca (with its label Argo) were taken over in 1980 and Harley Usill who had founded Argo split away to form 'a brand new label to reflect Argo's enterprising flavour'. Their early releases included titles from the Enigma list; in 1987 they set up the Quicksilva label ('A priceless compact disc series at an LP price'), on which many Northern Sinfonia recordings were to be reissued.

It has been possible to reconstruct the Sinfonia's discography pretty fully, though with over 100 titles it has proved too large for inclusion here. Some memorable examples can at least be commented on…

## The Brandenburg Concertos

A full set of concertos 1–6 was recorded with George Malcolm as conductor and harpsichordist, and issued by ASV on LP in 1977 (later reissued on CD). The recordings were made in All Saints, Quayside – a quiet venue with a 'nice clean sound.' Academy Sound and Vision were delighted with the result, and issued it as a double LP; distributed via the Britannia Record Club, it had excellent sales.

The performance marks an interesting stage in the rehabilitation of the Baroque (dating from at least the 1930s), by which we imply the shedding of 'Romantic' extrovert emotional conventions, and respect for the historic score. The result is impressive in its clarity and definition, and full of character, though the performance was made without the benefit of Baroque trumpets or the elaboration of cadenzas.

George Malcolm said of his approach:

> 'I come to Bach's music by the semi-Romantic approach which was still wide open in the 1920s of my childhood. Since those days we have all been taught a more authentic style of interpretation. I should like to think that my performance of the Brandenburgs with my friends of the Northern Sinfonia owes something to both of these very different traditions.' (sleeve-note)

A review in *Records & Recording*, September 1977 commented on the unexpanded 'slow movement' in no. 3, and the use of flutes for recorders in no's. 2 and 4 ('from an aesthetic preference' – Malcolm);

> '… otherwise there is a complete awareness of the Baroque style in all respects and superb solo playing, notably from John Wilbraham on trumpet in no. 2 and Malcolm himself as brilliant virtuoso harpsichordist in no. 5. Allegro movements all enjoy vivacious attack and springy rhythm, slow movements are deeply felt

without tipping over into romantic excess.'

The recording is also an affecting reminder of the status of these concertos in Northern Sinfonia's repertoire back in the 1960s and '70s, and the 'beautifully marked parts with bowing, phrasing and dynamics all shown' (*Friends News* Dec 1998) provided by George Malcolm. The works remain an important item of the current repertoire: Bach's 'six immortal Brandenburg Concertos' were a centrepiece of the 2003–04 rush-hour concerts...

## The Cycle of Beethoven Symphonies

This ambitious project was launched as part of the 25th anniversary season, when Hickox arranged with ASV to record, 'all the Beethoven symphonies played with orchestral forces in the proportions of the original performances.' (*Prospectus* 1983–84 p. 51)

The cycle was not recorded in order of composition: first came the 'Eroica' (no. 3), then the 'Pastoral' (no. 6), followed by no's. 1, 4 and 7. These spanned the years 1984–86, but then there came a pause, indeed the cycle had reached a point at which some were considering abandoning it altogether.

> 'The managing director of ASV had always recognised that a Beethoven symphonies cycle would sell slowly, but in view of his company's very good sales figures on other product(s) was anxious to prove to The Northern Sinfonia Trust (which is investing in the Orchestra's present recordings) that he can also sell the Northern Sinfonia. He had therefore proposed to keep faith with the Orchestra by going ahead with the recording of the second and eighth Beethoven symphonies as this was already in everyone's schedule, but to suspend the project at this point in favour of the *opus 6 concerti grossi* of Handel with George Malcolm in celebration of Mr Malcolm's 70th birthday.' (Man. Mins 29 Oct 1985)

The reissue on a budget price label of Karajan's Beethoven symphony cycle at that time can't have helped. However, the Northern Sinfonia project was not abandoned: Symphonies 5 and 9 were finally added in 1988, after sponsorship was forthcoming to finance the completion of the series, and arguably proved the best performances of all. (A note of May of that year tells us, 'the sell-out performances [of Beethoven 5 and 9] were immediately followed by recording sessions, thus completing the Sinfonia's Beethoven cycle on ASV.' (AGM 1989)

Due to the time span, different recording venues were used: the 'Eroica' was played in King's Hall, Newcastle University; Symphony no. 7 in Trinity Hall, Northumberland Road; whereas no's. 5 and 9 were recorded in the more resonant All Saints, Quayside.

There are many recordings of the Beethoven symphonies available, and none, arguably, can be deemed definitive. It is doubtful therefore whether the whole set of Hickox recordings will remain available, but there are some truly memorable performances among them – not least the fifth and ninth. The symphonies themselves are a 'Wonder of the World' there is no need to travel to far-off lands to appreciate; Hickox' contribution was summarised as follows in Northern Sinfonia's *Music* magazine:

> 'One of Richard's aims with the Sinfonia was to perform the music of each era more authentically. This was an aim in keeping with international developments in performing practice, but, as well as following a trend, Richard and the Sinfonia helped to set it, as in their recordings of the Beethoven symphonies – the first complete cycle to use the historically correct proportions of strings, woodwind and brass.' (May–Jul 2003)

## Albert Herring

Britten's 'Albert Herring' (conducted by Steuart Bedford) was recorded for Collins in 1997. This was Britten's third opera (after 'Peter Grimes' and 'The Rape of Lucretia'), composed in 1947 to a libretto of considerable wit by Eric Crozier that moves happily from prose to set pieces (ballad, song, aria, etc.) without undue subservience to rhyme.

Britten designed this as a chamber opera, and gave it a light, inventive orchestration, with a typically large role for the percussion section. Much of the text is set as recitative, with piano subtending the voice, but there are also many effective ensembles, and Britten was well aware of the satirical potential the libretto offered him ('Quite nicely sung, but rather modern, wasn't it?' is one of Lady Billows' lines).

The singers are convincingly dead-pan in their beautifully preposterous roles, while the verve and sparkle of the instrumental playing helps bring out the underlying humour – not only at the expense of the England of 1900 but doubtless of post-war pomposity too. Highly recommended!

## The Chopin Piano Concertos

To round off this section, and as something of a contrast of scale, it is well worth including Tamás Vásáry's playing/directing of the two Chopin piano concertos (issued by ASV in 1983 and produced by Antony Sargent, who nearly two decades later was to return to Northern Sinfonia as General Director at their new home The Sage Gateshead). These have a nervous excitement, a controlled energy and lyrical sensitivity that can indeed be said to bring the score 'to life'. Paradoxically the success may owe something to the inclement North East weather. The second concerto was recorded at The Sinfonia Centre on a 'desperately cold and wintry day' – snow fell in the afternoon so the players were left dependent on a local shop for snacks during their afternoon break instead of going further afield for refreshment. Returning to the relative warmth of the studio, with wits sharpened by the weather, they made the final complete play-through, which (unusually in the recording world) was used intact for the master.

# Chapter Four
## Logistics, outreach, education and advance

*'I for one had dreamed of a golden elixir, a magic book containing the secrets of the music profession's mystery.'*

Keith Statham in 1970–71 *Prospectus*.

## Logistics

'Running an orchestra on a day-to-day basis is a process of kaleidoscopic complexity,' it was noted in the Sinfonia publication *Inside Story* (1992). It has meant a periodic review of the roles needed of administrative officers.

In nearly all orchestras across the world overall executive responsibility is vested in the General Manager (or 'Chief Executive'). In the early days of Northern Sinfonia it was viola player, Antony Cullen, who first held the title. As recalled later in the *Friends Newsletter* (Jun 1998):

> 'His duties included booking halls and players, arranging transport and publicity, assisting in the arranging of programmes, obtaining the music, paying the players, keeping the Society's books – with a little help from the bank – and helping to set up the platform.'

(As well as playing!)

Latterly, the General Manager (or Chief Executive) would supervise and bear responsibility for the management and administration, and in particular handle the artistic contacts that shape the work of the orchestra.

In the 1960s some of the General Manager's work passed to his second-in-command, the Concert Manager, a post held by Tony Froud from 1967 to 1989. The duties were given as follows:

> 'Firstly, the venue for the concert is checked to ensure that the platform, lighting and heating are all in order and also that the stewards, programme sellers and box-office are laid on for that concert. Out of this arises the question of ticket agencies and these are arranged and kept informed of any intricacy in booking such as special rates for children, old age pensioners and parties. Tickets are customarily printed from this office and the prices of seats are arranged in conjunction with the local agent. Seating plans of all halls are carefully worked out in order to produce a

maximum gross without excessive top prices; this naturally depends on the size of the hall and the type of public liable to come to the concert.

Secondly, publicity is then worked out, usually with the co-operation of the ticket agents themselves or a local person who is willing to help as in the case of Carlisle. It has been my custom to go over in advance to the relevant town and work out with the agent what is best in the publicity line. Publicity is then ordered from the printers and as soon as it is ready it is circulated to the agents for distribution according to our previous discussion. This publicity may take the form of posters (double crown size posters are usually displayed by a poster service), hanging cards and leaflets. The office is responsible for the design and lay-out of this material and for ensuring that the cost of producing and displaying is within the budget allowed for the concert...' (Man. Mins 28 Apr 1965)

Budgeting was indeed a key word. The first full-time accountant, Jimmy Gilhespie, was succeeded by Gerry Hogarth in 1977, who worked with the Sinfonia for 22 years till 1999. In 1977, accounts were kept manually, planning only one year ahead, until Gerry Hogarth supervised the introduction of computers that made it more practical to forecast and plan up to three years ahead.

Another necessary and important figure is the Orchestra Manager, a sort of 'dean of the orchestra' or immediate point of contact between the players and management. His role is, 'ensuring that the right people are in the right place in the right dress at the right time.' (Tony Froud) As Anthony Brice (Orchestra Manager since 2002) notes in the *Friends Newsletter*, it involves,

'... booking extra musicians for all the of the concerts as well as being responsible for the majority of the arrangements for each concert... looking after Northern Sinfonia musicians... helping Ray [Wright] to change the layout of the orchestra before, during and after the performance.'

Co-operating with the Orchestra Manager is the Librarian, who looks after the scores the orchestra needs for each concert. This post was created in 1961, with Crawford Massey, Sinfonia violinist, taking on the role. As Tony Froud recalls:

'... Crawford learned when to hire and when to buy music, and, in each case, from whom; how to track down music which did not feature in easily-accessible publisher's lists; and to keep the immaculate records of all that he did, with whom and what it cost. Over the years he cultivated the friendship of just about every orchestral and music publisher's librarian, and built up one of the finest libraries of orchestral and chamber music owned by any orchestra in the country. And this library, incidentally, he used, until The Sinfonia Centre was built, to keep in his own home! But there is more to a librarian's work. Not only has the music to be ordered – in some cases tracked down – it has then to be prepared, and to be ready in time. Some conductors want their own markings pencilled into parts in advance of rehearsals; these will then usually have to be erased before the parts go back into the library. Just occasionally complete material is not available, and one would discover Crawford painstakingly creating a score from the parts, or vice versa. Score and parts then have to be on the desks for the start of rehearsals...' (*Friends News* Mar 2001)

Fortunately, organisational matters usually ran smoothly, and a little of the credit for the Orchestra's well-being must surely go to the secretary to the General Manager. The popular and admirably competent Isabel Whitelaw originally occupied this post, until her retirement in 1981. In 1983, Geraldine Bruce also retired, having,

'... served the Society long and devotedly for many years, running the block-bookings box office for children's concerts, manning the switchboard, typing letters, invoices and press releases, being kind to everyone and indefatigably producing tea or coffee for all visitors.' (*Friends News* Autumn 1984)

Luckily, an equally personable and effective team of two – familiar to many current supporters of the Orchestra – took on the secretarial work:

'Alison Manwell and Jean Sussman have served on the staff of the Sinfonia since 1980. When the post of secretary to the General Manager fell vacant, they took on the position on a job-share basis... [until] they [both] retired in 2003. They witnessed the change from manual typewriter to electric typewriter, to computer, during a modernisation of the management and the Sinfonia every bit as remarkable. Duties included ferrying soloists to and from hotels and supervising the box office as well as secretarial work...' (*Friends News* Aug–Oct 2003)

They were also the kind helpers who set this book going, with their useful list of contacts, introductions and suggestions.

Then there are the practicalities of transport for the more cumbersome instruments when Northern Sinfonia played away from home. In the early days of the Orchestra, a Primrose coach driver, George Nixon, took on this challenge, originally transporting players to concerts here and abroad (an image of him driving the original Primrose vehicle is preserved in the BBC film of 1966). He then joined the Sinfonia staff, taking on the role of 'Tours Manager', which included booking hotels as well as handling transport. He proved a popular figure.

Remembered by the players as a 'great character' and a pleasant and helpful (one might say essential) member of the Orchestra, something of the work he put in can be judged from a small note in the Finance Committee minutes for 16 September 1969:

'Mr. Nixon recommended that the Society should exchange its van since the present vehicle had done 50,000 miles in two years and its essential reliability was now becoming questionable.'

In 1986, the Sinfonia were lucky to find Ray Wright to take over when George retired, with the new title of 'Orchestral Attendant', reflecting his main responsibility of transporting the Orchestra's instruments and equipment in the Sinfonia's 22-foot Sprint van. (Players would use their own transport locally, or travel by a separate hired coach.) Ray needed to be on-site several hours before the players, when his job was to set up the stage for the Orchestra, position music stands and music, move the timpani and double-basses into position, arrange seating for the players, and check the lighting on stage (the rule being 'lighting must be overhead and fade-able and musicians looking up at the conductor should never experience glare.') This is somewhat easier in the big concert halls, where music stands and the like will be provided; but then there is often some rearrangement of the stage needed during a concert. For Northern Sinfonia concerts in its new home, the design of The Sage Gateshead will make a welcome change, with loading bays and stages all on one level.

Transport becomes even more of a responsibility when the Orchestra play abroad. For the Continent, Ray takes the instruments and equipment by sea and land, while players (nowadays) usually fly. The arrival of the Common Market has led to some easing of frontier controls: instead of the old-fashioned detailed 'carnets' to authorise entry and exit of goods, 'now you can just toddle through without being stopped at all!' (Ray Wright, Archive 7/8)

And then? As Alison Manwell, secretary to the General Manager, commented:

'Once the Orchestra has left the country we pray that we will not receive any faxes or phone calls informing us of any problems which may have arisen and prepare for concerts in this country for the Orchestra's return. It is likely that we will continue working on future tours – the process never ends!' (*Friends News* ca.1992)

## Funding and fundraising

Of that least ethereal commodity, money, Keith Statham noted in 1971, 'In any of the performing arts, quality depends on it.' (*Prospectus* 1970–71 p. 4) The operation of an orchestra is not of the kind that generates a profit; even a concert is not the guaranteed source of income we might suppose:

> 'Promotions – performances which the Society itself promotes – are the main vehicle by which the Orchestra reaches its audiences and establishes its identity within the region. Regular promotions assure regular rehearsal and performances under the Society's artistic control, and therefore remain a continuing policy.
>
> Engagements, within the region or elsewhere, are performances where the Orchestra is engaged at a fee by another promoter. The policy is to generate outreach and income, subject to the maintenance of quality. Whatever the nature of the engagement, the intention is to project the standard and identity of the Orchestra.' (Corporate Plan 1988–91)

Depending on costs and attendance levels, promotional concerts always involve a financial risk. At the very beginning, generous donations from Sir Humphrey Noble kept the accounts in credit; but such individuals are real rarities, and in 1968, 'The Chairman explained that the Society wanted, needed and, at the insistence of the Arts Council was in any case compelled, to raise a reserve fund.' (Man. Mins 29 May 1968)

Apart from dealing with unforeseeable contingencies, the practical application of this approach became apparent when funds were needed to build the new Sinfonia Centre in Jesmond Vale. Appeals to individuals, to businesses, and to large civic arts and other trust bodies for special project grants worked successfully to raise the major part of the capital needed.

On the completion of the Sinfonia Centre Appeal, the need for extra capital funding was not diminished, for 'there are many things which would benefit the Society for which extra money is needed' (Finance Mins 26 Mar 1979) – including benevolent applications, sponsorships of recordings, overseas tours and UK concerts...

Accordingly The Northern Sinfonia Trust was set up at the 1980 AGM as a separate legal entity, with the Marquis of Londonderry as patron, to raise capital which would be used, 'for the promotion and development of the Orchestra and to provide a buffer against financial crisis.' (*Friends News* Autumn 1985) A new Development Fund Appeal with a target of £250,000 was launched by the Trust in 1992, and proved an essential fail-safe for the Orchestra in coming years, as well as helping to promote education and outreach, recordings, a more extensive schedule of tours, and special projects like Young Sinfonia.

It acted as a spur for supporters of the Sinfonia to organise their own fund-raising activities, to the benefit of trust funds.

## The Viennese balls

The series of Viennese Balls for which the Orchestra has become well-known was initiated in 1978 and is generally held in November to keep it clear of the busy Christmas/New Year period. It has become a Sinfonia tradition in its own right:

> 'The glittering social occasion in the crown of the Sinfonia Year, offering good food, good wine and good company – together with the delicious opportunity to dance the Viennese waltz to the romantic strains of Northern Sinfonia.' (AGM 1989)

These balls are organised by the Ladies Committee. As the present Chair, Val Jobe, explained:

> 'The Ladies Committee was formed in 1978 by Lilly Harris, who was then Friends Secretary. Lilly had the idea to hold a Viennese Ball to raise funds for the Orchestra. To help her in the task she enlisted a few personal friends and committed Sinfonia supporters and together they organised the first ball. This was held on a Monday, the only evening available at Newcastle Civic Centre. The evening was a huge success raising £1,000, which was a considerable sum then. The ball became an annual event and was sponsored first by Reg Vardy (for about eight years); other sponsors have included IBM, Arthur Anderson, PriceWaterhouseCoopers (and most recently Robert Muckle Solicitors).' (*40 Years*)

The typical pattern of the evening was a gourmet three-course meal, followed by dancing to the music of the Strauss family, played by Northern Sinfonia, varied perhaps by a solo singer or instrumentalist; alternating with a modern band catering for more recent dance fashions.

For example, here is the line-up for 1994:

| | |
|---|---|
| 7.00 pm: | Reception with wine |
| 7.45: | Dinner – a three-course meal followed by coffee and mints |
| 9.00: | Bradley Creswick on violin (playing some Gipsy 'fiddle' music) |
| 9.15–10.00: | Northern Sinfonia play Viennese music for dancing, conducted by Alan Fearon |
| 10.00–10.45: | Fairwind 'The big band sound' |
| 10.45: | Grand draw |
| 11.00–12.00: | Northern Sinfonia (ending with the 'Donner und Blitzen' Polka and the 'Blue Danube' Waltz) |
| 12.00–1.00: | Fairwind |
| 1.00 am: | Carriages. |

Though costs must have been considerable, so were ticket prices, and this once-a-year special occasion ('attracting at least some people not in the normal Sinfonia "circle"') generated a considerable contribution to Sinfonia funds: the news that the Ladies Committee had raised £10,000 for the Sinfonia Trust through their Viennese Ball was greeted with well-deserved applause at the 1986 AGM.

In the 1990s the Viennese Balls were often announced as fund-raising events for specific purposes: in 1994, in aid of the Northern Sinfonia Instrument Bank and in 1995, in aid of Young Sinfonia – a useful reminder of the good causes behind all the swirl and glitter.

In due course, encouraged by the success of this type of entertainment and its positive contributions to the Orchestra's finances, the Ladies Committee decided to expand its activities, and in 1984 a 'Summer Evening' in the Great Hall of Alnwick Castle was introduced, that featured stars like Thomas Allen, Sheila Armstrong and Sarah Walker. Alternatively there might be a 'Summer Ball' at Wynyard Hall (the former seat of the Londonderry family) – noted in 1988 as, 'A splendid occasion!' (Man. Mins 7 Jul 1988)

Then:

> 'We decided to take advantage of a "free" venue, the rehearsal hall at The Sinfonia Centre, to hold more fund-raising evenings, and came up with the idea of evenings linking the music and food of a particular country. Alan Fearon has been a star of these events. We name the country, he does the research and finds the music...'

> This series included an Italian evening in 1989 and in 1990 an Austrian evening with chamber music by members of the Sinfonia and 'a sumptuous Austrian supper' – with all proceeds going to The Northern Sinfonia Trust.

> Not perhaps the usual enterprise we associate with the orchestral round, but, 'certainly when we see the figures (we raise on average £20,000 a year) we feel quite satisfied!' (*40 Years*)

## Friends of the Sinfonia

Friends of the Sinfonia – 'the Orchestra's "supporters" club' – has successfully served, over the years, to assist with fundraising and to provide a channel of contact between the admirers and the Orchestra itself

Its origin is described in a *Friends Newsletter* of 1988:

> 'The members of the Society have always supported the Orchestra faithfully since it was formed in 1958. It wasn't, however, until March 1979 that Gwen Polwarth volunteered to set up a members organisation, with the aim of increasing audiences and subscribers. It was also at this time that members became known as "Friends", in a move to make being a member of the Society more interesting with the introduction of such things as "Friends Evenings" and Newsletters, etc.'

The use of The Sinfonia Centre as a venue for meetings was a great help, and since then, Friends groups have developed in Newcastle and Carlisle, and more recently on Teesside, with a total membership now of around 500. Their lively newsletter alerts members to what is forthcoming and notable in the Sinfonia's schedule (including broadcasts and recordings), and provides news of the Orchestra, its past, present and plans. Jim Craigie has been responsible for much of the content of the *Friends Newsletter* over the years, including a series of interviews with players and staff that has given the *Newsletter* an added personal dimension. It is an especially welcome method of keeping in touch for those who now live out of the area or are otherwise unable to attend concerts regularly.

As well as maintaining contact by post, the Friends of the Sinfonia mount special evening events featuring a chamber music performance or talk about music, with a chance to meet and talk to each other (and the musicians) over refreshments – a delightful way of breaking down the formal barrier that usually exists between players and audience, as well as bringing the members of the audience into closer social contact with each other.

One memorable evening, recalled by current Friends' Chair, Audrey Butterworth, featured Sir Michael Tippett talking about how he composed, giving illustrations at the piano. It included a question and answer session, much appreciated by the large audience, which included many music students from the University of Durham.

Perhaps more typically, an evening will be a recital by members of the Orchestra itself, or arranged via contacts within Northern Sinfonia. For Friends in Newcastle in 2003, for example, this meant excellent performances of Dvořák's Terzetto and Kodaly's Serenade for String Trio, and violin sonatas by Isaye and Brahms, in just two of the many performances planned throughout the region for the 2003–2004 season.

Sometimes treats come unexpectedly to the volunteers who prepare the tempting array of refreshments. Barbara Westoll recalls an 'idyllic' afternoon at the Sinfonia Centre, preparing sandwiches for a Friends evening, when John Lill turned up, hungry after driving up from London, and keen to sample the fare. He was due to play and talk to the Friends that evening and give a concert with Northern Sinfonia the next evening. Refreshed he sat down to practise at the piano, while Barbara carried on her preparations – it was just like her own special private concert!

The organisation of these events continued on a voluntary basis until Joyce Porter switched to become employed as part-time Friends Co-ordinator in 1995, in recognition of the volume of work involved. Her efforts in maintaining and extending the activities of the Friends have been highly appreciated and anyone attending their events cannot fail to be struck by, 'the special, relaxed atmosphere, which combines with the quality of musical performances to make for very appealing occasions.' (Andrew Bennett, Chief Executive, Dec 2000)

## Outreach

'Outreach' implies a special effort to involve the community in the activities and opportunities offered by Northern Sinfonia, beyond the normal concert series and outside the main urban centres. Concerts in smaller towns have been an important feature of this work, reaching those who might not easily travel to the main concert venues. For example, in the 1983–84 season, besides 14 main concerts in Newcastle, eight in Carlisle and four each in Middlesbrough, Stockton and Darlington, there were also concerts in Hexham, Kendall, Penrith, Hartlepool, Bishop Auckland, Consett, Tynemouth and Cleveland.

Such work outside the main conurbations is usually specifically grant-aided as it involves smaller audiences and orchestral forces, but no significant reduction in administration, travel and other expenses.

*Penrith residency (1983–84)*

As for cutting costs, it became a maxim that smaller venues must not mean lower standards, and the Finance Committee had pledged itself to the highest quality of performance and best performers in the smallest town engagements, so that, 'the Orchestra not only was, but was seen to be, performing at the same level whether in Berlin or Bishop Auckland.' (Finance Mins 6 Nov 1979)

The solution to the economic challenge has lain in flexibility: the provision of concerts scaled to suit local halls and local audiences, in keeping with financial good sense, without diminution of quality. As Anthony Phillips, the Music Officer of Northern Arts, reported vividly in 1971:

> 'Not only does the full Orchestra play in most towns of any size in our region, but (its ensembles) reach smaller communities which a few years ago would have expected live concerts like they would have expected someone to strike oil in the village green.' (*Prospectus* 1970–71 p. 54)

In the mid-1980s, the Arts Council's 'Glory of the Garden' scheme allowed the Orchestra to put in for six additional string players to increase their options: with a large body of strings, two or three ensembles could be formed to carry out smaller-scale regional commitments. This enabled an expanded series of 'Village Halls Tours' which then included coverage of Northumberland (where the Orchestra 'reached a new and enthusiastic public; it offered access, understanding and enjoyment' – *Inside Story*); and a Yorkshire and Humberside 'Rural Tour' in June 1994 (playing at Flamborough, Driffield and Beverley).

This useful initiative became known as the Sinfonia's 'Summer Roadshow':

> 'The Sinfonia is committed to spending at least one week a year out on the road, taking live music of the very highest standard to local communities. This year (1997) sees us covering the whole breadth of the region, from Saltburn on the East coast to Crosscanonby on the West coast...' (*brochure* 1997)

The annual Lakeland tour became a regular event, starting in 1973, and taking in such towns as Grizedale, Keswick, Norham, Penrith and Whitehaven. The tenth tour in July 1982 was especially memorable, with George Malcolm as soloist in harpsichord and piano concertos. In 1998, in association with National Orchestra Week, the Sinfonia's visit to Penrith took the form of a residency (10–13 March), not the usual concert format but, 'informal performances and music workshops in the community' involving playing and composition opportunities based on ideas from Haydn, Stravinsky, Bartók and sea shanties, with local choirs working on some of the projects; showing something of the potential for extending contact into participation.

**The Robert Mayer Children's Concerts**

Education is now fully recognised as an equally essential aspect of outreach. This has taken many forms: 'school hall' concerts, classroom workshops, school projects, and back in the 1960s, a series of larger scale performances at a central locale.

Concerts for children were pioneered by Sir Robert Mayer before World War Two – including some in Newcastle. In March 1968, Keith Statham approached Sir Robert with a view to running a new series for under-14s on Saturday mornings at the City Hall, and these were in place by the autumn of that year. Reasonably priced tickets were offered to ensure large parties from schools in the region; though this precluded a profit, Sir Robert himself provided a guarantee against loss. They were by all accounts exciting and musically rewarding events. Northern Sinfonia Chairman Charles Brackenbury reported of them, '... the City Hall was full with a really magnificent and wonderful audience which showed its appreciation in no unmeasured terms.' (AGM 1969)

As the founder explained:

> 'Robert Mayer Concerts for Children is a national movement which was launched by Lady Mayer and myself 50 years ago. It has succeeded in making millions of children love music; widening their musical

knowledge; encouraging them to make music themselves and acquiring early in life the habit of concert-going, which is essential for their future and the growth of Newcastle's musical life. The low price of admissions, specially arranged programmes and explanatory talks during the performances are added attractions.' (*Prospectus* 1970–71 p. 15)

Too much like a school lesson? The *Prospectus* for the 1970–71 season gave assurances to the contrary:

'During the past two seasons over 9,000 children have attended the Robert Mayer Concerts for Children presented by the Northern Sinfonia Orchestra and for the coming season we hope that the concerts listed on the back page will create a similar excitement.

The concerts will all take place in the City Hall, Newcastle, at 11 o'clock on the Saturday mornings shown and will be introduced by Clifford Barratt, the

Music Adviser to Gateshead Education Authority. We hasten to add that Mr Barratt's presence does not mean that his remarks will be in any way like a school lesson but he will simply be giving the children a few general pointers about the pieces they will hear...'

For the 1970–71 season these Sinfonia concerts were conducted by David Haslam – he also composed some of the music to be played! The emphasis was on music with a story, but there were also useful demonstrations of individual instruments and their capabilities.

After a long run, the children's concerts came under pressure in 1983. For one thing, 'music teachers were extremely busy people who could not take on extras such as organising parties to concerts...' (AGM 1983) There were so many other activities to occupy children's time, that the concerts somehow got squeezed out in the mid-1980s. However, it would not be possible to say goodbye without remembering one particular star of the series...

Robert Mayer Children's Concerts (1970–71)

*Johnny Morris*

### Johnny Morris and Northern Sinfonia

As many of the concerts for children were based on the concept of 'stories with music', it is not surprising that Northern Sinfonia soon teamed up with that story-teller par excellence and popular children's TV personality, Johnny Morris.

Initially he had been invited to supply the narrator's part for 'Peter and the Wolf', but as he recalled later, that was to be just the start:

'The Northern Sinfonia and the "Hot Chestnut Man" worked pretty well. Had I got anything else? Well I had. Some years before I had a story which Sidney Sagar had set to music. It was called "Delilah the Sensitive Cow". It was a Big Bang Ding Dong Wallop sort of piece, but it was funny and a carefree bit of fun. Had I got anything else? Alas and alack no! Then up spoke a young tousled flute player named David Haslam. "You write the story," he challenged "and I'll write the score!" So I wrote "Juanita the Spanish Lobster" and David turned in a most brilliant score. These pieces, and there were six in all, lasted about 20 minutes and they formed the basis for the children's concerts that happened on Saturday mornings at Newcastle City Hall and at the Playhouse.' (*40 Years*)

As well as forming part of the Saturday morning concerts, the performances were adapted for television by Tyne Tees Television, and some animation sequences added. Johnny Morris remained central to the action (occasionally flexing his fine tenor singing voice), and the need for accuracy can be gauged by the marking up of this excerpt from the script of 'Johnny meets the strings and tells the story of –

### M4 THE MOTORWAY or BOUNCER THE FROG

Duration: 17 mins approx

CUES HAVE BEEN CHECKED. ONE OR TWO CUTS IN THE SCRIPT AS WELL.

WORDS UNACCOMPANIED BY MUSIC INDICATED BY INVERTED COMMAS

\*\*\*\*\*\*\*\*\*\*\*\*\*\*\*\*\*\*\*\*\*\*\*\*\*\*\*\*\*\*\*\*

(7' GENTLE FLUTE INTRODUCTION)

Once upon a time

(7' MUSIC)

there was a monster.

(15' MONSTER THEME FROM A WITH TIMPS)

It tramped slowly through the countryside
banging and thumping and smashing down the
spiky trees and sucking up the pools and the ponds.

*Clarinet tune*

Ripping up the green grass meadows, tearing
down the hedgerows, driving people from their
homes and terrifying the animals for miles around. (27')

It was a motorway

(12' MUSIC)

and when it had gobbled up all the countryside
it needed, it just lay down quietly and let the
traffic go up and down its roads, all night and day.

(8' TRAFFIC EFFECTS, MOTOR HORN)

'The animals soon learned that the motorway
wouldn't harm them as long as they kept away
from it, but to try to cross the motorway
they knew meant certain death. And every evening
every animal mother and father sang to their
children of the deadly dangers of the motorway.' (23')'

(Archive 2/9/1)

(Of course, young Bouncer won't be warned, and attempts to hop across. He looks very likely to be flattened when a junior barn owl (who isn't quite ready to kill anything) swoops and picks him up and drops him back safe in his home pond.)

Like all good things, the Morris-Haslam collaborations came to an end. At an executive meeting of 26 June 1986, Northern Sinfonia faced up to it: 'Johnny Morris was becoming somewhat out of touch with the modern child…' The world of coal-fires, chestnuts, and *Children's Hour* was fast disappearing…

However, the cause of children's concerts was not forgotten, and in 1989 the Sinfonia launched 'Saturday Superset', 'a new approach to family concerts at the Newcastle Playhouse, introduced and conducted by Richard McNicol.' (AGM 1989) In 1995, Melvin Tix the magical, musical clown made his first appearance with the Sinfonia in concerts for children. His story reads like one of Johnny Morris's best:

'Petter Vabog was born in Sandefjord, near Oslo in Norway. When he was six years old he was given his first recorder. He learned how to read music score [sic] and played all day! Two years later he joined the Boys Band and started to play the alto horn. In the beginning the sounds he made were like those of a hungry cow! Petter practised very hard and when he was 10 years old started to play the cornet and later the french horn – the hungry cow is now gone! As Petter grew up he had lots of music lessons and joined the Armed Services Band.

Eventually he studied at the Norwegian Academy of Music and became the principal horn player in the Stravanger Symphony Orchestra. In 1979 Petter was bitten by the magic bug and became a member of the Magic Circle, then Melvin Tix was 'born'… the first and only magical, mystical clown in Norway!'
(NS programme 5 Feb 1995)

## Education

As the Northern Sinfonia Corporate Plan announced in 1988: 'Education is… central to its objective to promote and advance the performance and appreciation of music.' Indeed, from its inception, Northern Sinfonia has been aware of the need to encourage a broader role for music in education, and help give pupils from the infants upwards some experience of live music and involvement in music-making. This has become a particularly important element in the plans for The Sage Gateshead, which is providing the opportunity to greatly expand the Orchestra's work across the full educational sphere from pre-school to Higher Education.

Before any note of music had been played, at the Orchestra's outset, Michael Hall had vowed to the Newcastle Corporation that, 'any surplus made will be

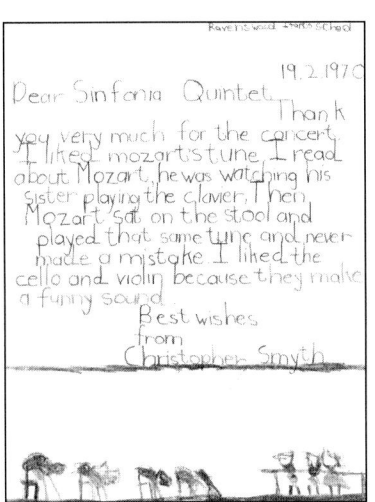

used to improve the Orchestra and give concerts to the schoolchildren in the city.' (Archive 7/12) The first fruits of this were some five concerts in schools in 1961. Such work depended necessarily on the co-operation of the County Councils as responsible for education, and received an uneven response from the authorities; Michael Hall recalls that Cumberland and Middlesbrough were especially keen on these early ventures.

With little or no surplus from the Sinfonia's own budget to finance educational visits, the continuance of school concerts came to depend absolutely on subsidy from Local Education Authorities. By the late 1960s Keith Statham was aware of the balance of issues here when he pointed out, 'that money available for education concerts was very limited and... we were in fact subsidising Education Authorities.' (Man. Mins 22 Jan 1968) During the 1970s and early 1980s, a series of larger-scale concerts for schoolchildren, mounted in Newcastle City Hall, were the preferred medium of contact.

Visits to schools also continued, for example in 1988: 'School groups, player-led, usually consisting of a string quartet with one, two or three wind players make 45 minute visits to schools...' (Corporate Plan 1988–91) Such sessions would not be so much recitals as workshops, 'taking themes from music and making them accessible to children.' (*Inside Story*) Four or so players proved an ideal formula, allowing the Sinfonia resources to divide and cover three schools simultaneously; the emphasis would be on demonstration and explanation rather than the more passive playing/listening approach.

The need for better co-ordination in the rather chance take-up of educational projects began to be addressed in 1990 when the Sinfonia appointed an Outreach Officer to organise their work in the community more effectively. Members of the Orchestra were ready to participate in educational schemes as part of their employment, and an ambitious series of projects involving the young of all levels of proficiency was put in place in recognition of the important role music can play in general education. The work still needed to be financed, and funding was provided partly by the schools and partly by sponsorship. Fortunately there was a growing consensus on the benefits of music for young people and this aspect of Northern Sinfonia's work has fast become its most significant role outside the concert hall.

The renewed educational activity was summarised in 1994 as composition and performance-based workshops in schools with associated teachers' workshops; outreach workshops, e.g. for people with learning difficulties and disabilities; and training initiatives for players, teachers and care staff.

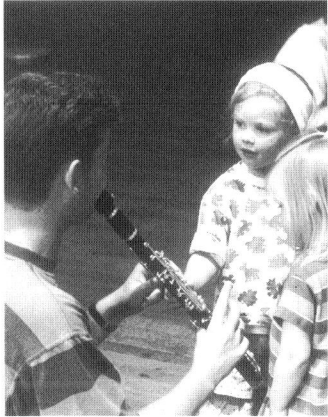

Educational benefits there would be – 'access to new experiences,' aimed at 'increasing and enhancing existing musical knowledge and appreciation' – but 'most importantly it promotes enjoyment.' (*Inside Story*) There was to be no lack of challenge for the children, however, and collaboration with composers and animators were exciting features in the programme.

The sort of projects that have developed since are well worth mentioning.

In 1993, the Northern Sinfonia,

'... teamed up with schools from across Northumberland and Newcastle to take part in a national education project "Turn of the Tide". The project included performing a specially composed piece by Sir Peter Maxwell Davies.' (NS brochure)

'Turn of the Tide' was then a major new initiative for environmental improvement on the North East coastline.

In 1997, Sinfonia musicians led a performance at Elvet Methodist Church in Durham City as part of the Miners Gala, the culmination of a project called 'Gala Gigs' in which pupils of four Durham schools worked with five members of Northern Sinfonia, 'to create their own musical contribution to the Gala.' (*Friends News* Jun 1997)

What we now know as The Sage Gateshead was, in embryo in 1999, the context for an ambitious three-year process of collaborative new music-making in Gateshead called 'Meteor Showers'. The first stage, called 'Starbirth', involved six workshops, including composition and vocal workshops at Ryton Comprehensive; a 'Discover the Trumpet' workshop at Ryton Junior School; and a music session for parents and toddlers at Bill Quay City Farm. This led up to a performance on 14 December at Caedmon Hall, Gateshead, when:

> 'We invited many different people – Gateshead schoolchildren, Northern Sinfonia musicians, writers, singers and instrumentalists – to come together in a collaborative mid-winter celebration, exploring the themes and textual messages of Handel's "Messiah" in a contemporary vein...' (Archive 2/11/10)

The performance was based on a sequence of poems, songs and instrumental pieces, mostly originating with the children working in small groups, with some of the instrumental music contributed by jazz composer Keith Morris.

The following year (Year 2) was called 'Life Time' and was based on, 'the different points of view that people of different ages have on the passage of time and the cycles of life'. Both A-level students and primary school children were involved in the preparations for a concert at the Dryden Centre.

The third part of this project was called 'Change' and culminated in a concert at the Dryden Centre on 17 December 2001 – 'a collage of words and music created and performed by Bill Quay Primary School, Blaydon Writers, Hookergate Young Musicians and musicians from Northern Sinfonia' – Clarence Adoo was one of the Northern Sinfonia players participating.

In a novel project, north of the river, Northern Sinfonia players Malcolm Critten, Alan Fearon and Bransby Roberts joined with furniture designer Adrian Sander to build a 'music machine' at Thomas Bewick School.

*Clarence Adoo*

*Roberto Carrillo-Garcia*

In Jim Craigie's words:

> 'Back in April this year (2000), a furniture designer arrived at a school in Chapel Park, Newcastle with a van full of scrap metal, springs, tubes and pieces of wood of all shapes and sizes... followed closely behind by musicians from Northern Sinfonia and a car load of percussion instruments. Three months later a wonderful "Sound Sculpture" appeared in the grounds of the school...' (*Friends News* Sep)

This was no mere gimmick or fantasia; the serious intention was to encourage pupils, especially those with communication difficulties, to explore,

> '... how different materials, shapes and sizes change sound and pitch and how even the most ordinary looking object can be played in many different ways. From this cacophony of sound and activity, Adrian was able to go away and build a practical and very elegant "Sound Sculpture", which was installed – in pouring rain – in time for the official opening of the school.' (*ibid.*)

Another education project in 2001 was led by animator Dee Isaacs:

> 'The project began with teachers from the participating schools painting a large canvas in response to ideas of foreground, background and texture. The resulting almost Chagall-like painting was then used as a stimulus for musical composition.' (*Friends News* 2001)

The schools participating were Whitley Bay High School and George Stephenson High School; the resulting score was performed by a Sinfonia wind quintet and cello, with some additional instruments played by pupils.

These enterprising examples can perhaps serve to illustrate the tremendous scope there is for involving music in practical projects within the education process

*Young Sinfonia with conductor Ilan Volkov (sitting second from right on bench)*

and for encouraging awareness of music at a level that is as basic or as sophisticated as the youngsters wish to make it.

## Young Sinfonia

The needs of the musically gifted child and the essential opportunity for them to play in a youth orchestra and gain experience of the concert world is something only too often outside the school curriculum. In 1959, schoolchildren Joy Towb and Richard Little put forward the case for a 'Junior Philharmonic' in the North East, and with a bit of adult expertise in organising it, a series of summer schools, culminating in public concerts, was initiated. This was a separate project from Northern Sinfonia, though Michael Hall was glad to undertake the early sessions of training and concert-making.

After the Junior Philharmonic encountered difficulties in the mid-1990s, a new opportunity for young players to practise together became a priority. What emerged was a new orchestra, to be named Young Sinfonia – a regional youth chamber orchestra directly associated with the Northern Sinfonia itself:

> 'The emphasis within Young Sinfonia is based on a professional approach to learning the skills required to play in a small orchestra... Over each academic year, from September to August, there is a balanced programme of activities that may include residential weekends and an international tour; public engagements and concerts; masterclasses and sectional rehearsals as well as weekly rehearsals of the full orchestra.'
> (YS *brochure* 2003–04)

Entry is by audition, with players aged 12 to 19 who have reached Grade VIII level eligible – a precondition necessary in view of the high standard of achievement aimed at in this venture, which gives able young musicians some idea of professional orchestral life and the opportunity to benefit from association with experienced players. As explained in their brochure:

> 'The Orchestra's close association with the Northern Sinfonia provides regular opportunities for sectional rehearsals and other sessions with players from the Northern Sinfonia and the international guest conductors, soloists and composers who work with them.'

The founding of Young Sinfonia owed much to a generous donation from Catherine Cookson; the early days of its formation were described as follows:

> 'Preparations for the new Young Sinfonia have been going on since summer 1995, and it was therefore very exciting to witness the Orchestra at its first gathering at the beginning of January (1996). Players from across the region had attended auditions in December, and those selected represent every county and include a double-bassist who travels from Kendal. Young Sinfonia was launched with an intensive weekend of rehearsals on 6–7 January, conducted by Alan Fearon and tutored by other members of Northern Sinfonia. Young Sinfonia is now rehearsing weekly on Sunday afternoons...' (*Friends News* 1996)

After a preliminary concert as part of the Brunswick Methodist Church concert series in March, the official inaugural concert took place as part of the Brinkburn Festival on Sunday 14 July 1996, at Brinkburn Abbey with Ilan Volkov conducting. The programme comprised Peter Maxwell Davies' 'Orkney Wedding with Sunrise', Mozart Symphony no. 31 (the 'Paris') and Stravinsky's 'Pulcinella Suite'.

This was followed by a summer tour of the French region of Limousin in mid-1997, and a tour of the Czech Republic in August 1998. A highlight of the latter was a concert in the Baroque church of St Nicholas, described here by a young player:

> 'It was very ornate and had a 1,400 kg chandelier in the centre of it which measured four metres across. The church also had large painted scenes on the ceiling and on the wall panels. The acoustic in the church gave us all a shock: as we played the first chord it went booming round and seemed to last for ages!' (*Friends News* Sep 1998)

A range of exceptional conductors was available to work with Young Sinfonia, thanks to the Arts Council's young conductor scheme, including Ilan Volkov, Andrei Danilov, Scott Stroman, Quentin Clare and Baldur Brönnimann (who reminded us, '... music in Young Sinfonia should be fun, should be about working together and exploring music, not about competition or pressure.' [*Friends News* Mar 2000])

High points have been recordings for BBC Radio 3 and Classic FM in 2001; premièring a piece commissioned from percussionist Peter Lockett at the WOW (Windows on the World) International Music Festival at North Shields in the same year; participating in 'The Royal Gala Concert' for Her Majesty the Queen at the opening of the Gateshead Millennium Bridge; and recording their first CD. The CD, called 'Building Bridges' was released in Autumn 2002: 'an eclectic mix of classical, jazz, folk – it's got it all.' (sleeve-note)

The administration of Young Sinfonia was taken on in 2001 by Marion Wilson (trumpet player with Northern Sinfonia); it is a project she has every reason to be proud of. As she reported in the *Friends Newsletter* for Aug–Oct 2003:

> 'Young Sinfonia finished its year with annual collaboration concerts with Northern Sinfonia in

Stockton and Newcastle. The concerts were of an exceptionally high standard and, as in past collaborations, Young Sinfonia members gained much from their experience of sitting next to their professional counterparts... Most of the solos were played by members of Young Sinfonia and without exception they all rose to the occasion and played beautifully. We have some very talented young musicians in the region...'

Young Sinfonia is now one of a group of youth ensembles, developed by The Sage Gateshead, that enable young players to experience the thrill and skills development associated with playing as part of a talented group of peers. Ensemble playing of this kind plays a central role in creating the professional musicians of the future. Some of Young Sinfonia's players also play in Folkestra (folk ensemble) or Jambone (the regional youth jazz ensemble) which broadens their musical horizons and aspirations.

And that important early training for hopeful musicians augurs well for the future of music in the North East.

## The Cobweb concept

This enterprising concept involving a wider sector of the community is non age-specific. Set up in 1995 by Andy Jackson, a ten-week project entitled 'Blow the Cobwebs off your Music Stand' was so successful, 'that it has become an on-going orchestra for amateur musicians of any age and any standard.' (*40 Years*)

The weekly rehearsal sessions and workshops were designed for,

> '... people who have only recently started to play an instrument, or who have not played for some time and would like to start again. Experienced players very welcome also!' (*NS brochure*)

After an enthusiastic start in County Durham, Cobwebs was extended to Cumbria and Northumberland, with

*Cobwebs concert*

support from the local councils. It now rehearses in three groups around the region on a weekly basis, the separate forces combining to give public concerts in liaison with experienced Sinfonia players.

Brahms' Second Symphony was the target for 1999, when,

> '... a "scratch" orchestra of 90 (including 10 musicians from the Northern Sinfonia) ranging in age from 19–70 and in ability from Grade 1 to professional met to rehearse and perform the symphony under the direction of Alan Fearon.' (*Friends News* Mar 1999)

There is plenty of enthusiasm for the opportunity to play in such harmonic company:

> 'Cobwebs has given people who haven't played since leaving full-time education the incentive to return to music-making, and others who have taken up an instrument in later life will find a welcoming and

encouraging environment in which to improve their skills.'(The Sage Gateshead website)

As Andy Jackson sums it up, 'it is about re-discovering the pleasure of music-making!'

**The Music Education Centre**

Education is a major focus of The Sage Gateshead project, with the new building including a Music Education Centre that can utilise specific rooms for teaching work at individual and group level, and of course excellent rehearsal space. It is a facility clearly needed considering the lack of any music conservatoire between Glasgow and Manchester.

Of particular usefulness to aspiring classical musicians will be the David Goldman Programme, set up in memory of former North East Business Man of the Year and founder of the accounting software company, Sage. This programme enables young players to take part in a number of musical activities including a Weekend School at The Sage Gateshead – a programme to include individual tuition on a particular instrument (or for voice), classes and workshops in musical theory, composition and conducting; participation in masterclasses; assistance with instrument hire or purchase. Tutors of the highest musical calibre, some of them Northern Sinfonia players, are employed to deliver the Weekend School programme and, of course, based at The Sage Gateshead will be the region's own youth ensembles including Jambone, Folkestra and Young Sinfonia.

Located at The Sage Gateshead, but with activities extending throughout schools and communities in the region, an exciting agenda for raising music awareness is in place. At the start of young lives there is a scheme for toddlers and parents groups, to get the children to try out making sound (simple percussion and singing), supervised by musicians from diverse musical backgrounds (orchestral, folk, improvised, and pop). This is an area of music education not well-developed until now, and the projects will include training for pre-school teachers, nursery supervisors and parents, 'to develop the skills and confidence to help them educate through music.'

At the other end of the educational lifecycle, a Higher Education Officer (Stuart Johnson) was appointed in 2002, a post' 'created jointly between the Universities for the North East and The Sage Gateshead… to establish enduring links between a major performing arts venue and the Higher Education sector.' (*NS Music* May–July 2003)

The intention is to provide extra options in undergraduate and postgraduate courses, including research work and training at a professional level. This has included setting up England's first Folk and Traditional Music degree programme, in partnership with Newcastle University.

These distinct projects are only three examples of the breadth and depth of music education that is being enabled on Tyneside by the multi-million pound project, The Sage Gateshead.

**A regional music centre**

A proposal for a new hall, at that stage sited in Newcastle was made by Northern Arts as far back as 1982, with the recommendation of a location on the Quayside; in 1986, a meeting on the 'Regional Concert/Conference Hall Feasibility Study' at Newcastle University (Archive 3/4/3) considered four options including the redundant Marlborough Crescent Bus Station near Central Station – though ultimately this favoured site attracted less support from local councillors and grant bodies than the Gateshead option. There was already, after all, Newcastle's City Hall, though it was less than ideal for the Sinfonia's purpose.

The City Hall of 1928 is centrally placed, has a capacity of some 2,200, but 'music could only be enjoyed satisfactorily from some 750 out of the 2,200 seats in the hall…' (Man. Mins 20 January 1969); Northern Arts confirmed that 'because of the design of the hall, the acoustics – particularly in certain parts – are extremely bad.'

(*The Journal* 25 Oct 1982)

Other criticisms have been:

> 'The soundproofing of the hall is poor... the alignment of the gallery seats is unsuitable, and the low level of the balcony floor prevents proper hearing from the seats beneath... The hall is cold for rehearsals... backstage accommodation is severely limited and overheated.' (Man. Mins 16 Jul 1968)

These problems had long been appreciated, but the call for a better facility had to await a new ethos of renewal on Tyneside.

In 1994, a report called *Creative Capital*, produced by Arts Business Ltd for Newcastle City Council, Northern Arts, the Newcastle Initiative and Newcastle Arts Forum, emphasised the importance of the cultural economy for Tyneside:

> 'The presence of good cultural facilities is a major factor in business confidence in a city, and it helps recruitment of senior personnel, investment and morale.'

It saw every reason for confidence that, 'the city will achieve its plans for major new facilities, such as a Concert Hall, new music training institution, new gallery space, further improved museums, and possibly a whole range of other new facilities.'

Capital funds would be available from the National Lottery as well as European and UK regeneration budgets, and better perhaps than any other Northern city, 'Newcastle is excellently placed to tap these.' In short, a major opportunity was identified to improve what we might call the artistic infrastructure and make it possible (as the Report concluded) for Tyneside to become, 'the distinctive, Creative Capital.'

The initiative was taken up by the Orchestra's management, who commissioned a report from John Myerscough; his 'New Concert Hall for Newcastle' (April 1994) established the feasibility of not only a concert hall but a wider-ranging concept – a Regional Music Centre.

The advantage of making this more than just a classical music facility was evident, bringing about a widening of both the partnership of music groups involved and the function of the building, to make it relevant to different music groups and the wider community. The most far-reaching of those partnerships was probably with Folkworks, the lively development agency for folk and traditional musics based in Newcastle but increasingly active nationally, who worked very closely with Northern Sinfonia in developing the Regional Music Centre idea, and 'in due course were – with the Sinfonia – to take up residence in The Sage Gateshead, fully integrated (like Sinfonia) into the management of their new home.' There were to be changes en route. An early suggestion of an exhibition gallery was not followed through, and the idea of a conference suite subordinated to the need for a coherent musical assemblage. Ideas like provision for teaching and a music library seemed sounder proposals.

Thus the project developed from a concert hall basis into a 'Regional Music Centre', where Northern Sinfonia would be the resident orchestra, but which would also provide teaching in music performance at all levels from starter courses to individual and group instruction for children of exceptional talent, university-level modules and courses for music teachers; there was to be a Northern Music and Theatre Library with regional remit, providing lending/reference services to the public in audio visual and print materials, as well as specialist support, and a major archive. The inclusion of the different musics of Tyneside was a major advantage in terms of attracting funding, for 'serious' music does not mean 'classical' exclusively: we are reminded of the early aspirations of the North East Association of the Arts (NEAA), whose 1962–63 Report advised extending funding to jazz and folk song. Bringing together compatible activities and music that could co-operate in terms of a single building could prove to be much to their mutual advantage.

It was this concept of a Regional Music Centre – 'a novel initiative in a British context' – which gave 'meaning' to the concert hall development, and did so much 'to convince public, local councils and grant authorities of the relevance and usefulness of the project.' At this stage a site west of Central Station was still being considered; but that did not unduly affect the detail of the project – the Myerscough Report continues:

> 'It will be a specialist hall of international standard with an outstanding natural acoustic dedicated in its operation to fostering music of all kinds. The Hall will be defined by a cultural and educational purpose in addition to its entertainment role.
>
> 'An auditorium of this capacity should enable acoustic excellence to be achieved with confidence. Arup Acoustics point out, that excellence in concert hall design requires dedication to concert use as the primary function. In halls which fail to provide adequate built volume and rely on electronic support to the sound there is an inevitable loss of quality. Newcastle should take advantage of the experience available to ensure that what is built provides for symphonic music at the highest level. With a capacity of 1,650, there is a wonderful chance to produce the very best.'

While the scale of seating was moderate (compared, say, to Newcastle City Hall at over 2,000)

> '... we believe a hall of this size and quality reflects emerging developments in the concert market. The scaling down in relation to the halls built in Britain in the 1980s is matched by similar developments elsewhere in Europe, especially in Scandinavia. The Concert Hall specification will be appropriate to the work of Northern Sinfonia, whilst remaining capable of mounting full-scale orchestral and choral concerts with acoustically thrilling results. Few seats in the Hall have less than the excellent vision and the acoustical immediacy which the modern concert goer expects.'

The design of this main hall was to benefit from experience in creating world class facilities for music in other parts of the world and would have an adjustable acoustic system based on advanced electronics, which will accommodate the various types of live and amplified music to be played there.

The Concert Halls are not to be the preserve in any sense of the Sinfonia, but to be used to 'foster music of all kinds.' Programming would be opened up to 'combine classical music, serious alternative music (jazz, folk, country and western, world music, rock/pop and middle of the road music), and comedy' in proportions: classical 62, serious alternative 25, others 65 (assuming a total of about 152 concerts a year).

The second (smaller) hall, accommodating some 450, would serve,

> '... both simple educational and rehearsal needs and provide for smaller scale public concerts. Events might include jazz, early music, music from Asia and other cultures, chamber music recitals and masterclasses (plus) lettings for meetings and other purposes.'

A versatile space!

A third performance space was to be integrated into the design, now known as Northern Rock Foundation Hall. This would be available,

> '... for rehearsal and performance to The Sage Gateshead's own and visiting musicians; students in the Music Education Centre, and local music organisations for performance and rehearsal, education and participative programmes.'

In addition to the above, The Barbour Room is a sunny space for events and entertainment with a capacity of up to 300.

Beside the Education Centre (already mentioned) there was planned the Northern Music and Theatre Library – a 'regional resource with lending, reference, archive and information services' filling a gap in such provision between Leeds and Edinburgh; it would 'aim to accumulate relevant archives on music and theatre (as) a gateway to existing information and... a collector of new materials.' Open to the general public, children, students and researchers, its core functions are seen as including 'lending of print and audio visual material; reference consultation; collecting and archiving (including recordings of performances)' as well as a point of access to outside resources. We may also mention here Farne (Folk Active Resource North East), a project of Gateshead Libraries, which in 2003 set about launching an internet site providing access to archive material about Northumbrian folk music from collections across the North East.

This whole reference facility was to be known in later plans as the Music Information Resource Centre (housed in the Joan and Margaret Halbert space), and to provide on-site and remote/online access to all kinds of practical, technical and historical music information, using new technology to revolutionise access to music and information about music.

The Myerscough Report concluded by outlining the possible operational basis: a development trust would run and maintain the building, and serve as a co-ordinating body for the three operating groups: the Concert Hall, Northern Sinfonia, and the Regional Music Centre (including Folkworks).

**Towards The Sage Gateshead**

The possibility of realising this brave ambition came a step closer with the award of a pilot 'stabilisation' grant to Northern Sinfonia from the Arts Council of Great Britain (funded by the National Lottery) in 1997. It was explained:

'The stabilisation programme was launched by the Arts Council a year ago. Its purpose is to strengthen arts organisations creatively, managerially and financially by providing them with the expert advice and financial resources to put them on a more secure financial footing.' (*Friends News* Sep 1997)

As regards Northern Sinfonia, this meant 'preparing the Society for its move into the RMC and... enabling a period of financial stability and artistic development.' With the keywords of 'Creativity, Teaching and Performance', and emphasis on marketing and new artistic and educational ventures, this programme fitted neatly the Orchestra's needs. Though not a capital grant towards the building itself, this funding was designed to prepare Northern Sinfonia for its new role in the Music Centre and provide a period of financial security and development during the transition.

Interestingly, segments of Newcastle Council had been unable to reach agreement about backing a new capital music resource, and the prime site west of Central Station became instead the International Centre for Life ('bioscience'). It was Gateshead Council that offered an obvious alternative and in many ways better site, on the fast regenerating quayside area that already housed BALTIC (planned to become an International Centre for Contemporary Visual Arts). Gateshead was in many ways an ideal local authority to deal with this project as unique among North East councils had retained an Arts Committee, even appointing a pioneer Arts Officer in 1982. Their considerable initiatives have included the new regional icon, The Angel of the North, and the concept of the Gateshead Millennium Bridge to directly link the north and south banks of the Tyne. Their offer of a prime riverside site for the new centre for music won against bids by Sunderland, North Tyneside and Chester-le-Street among others across the North to house the new project.

*Virtual reality image showing proposed inside of The Sage Gateshead.
Image courtesy of Foster and Partners.*

And so:

'Within four years the Northern Sinfonia will become the resident orchestra in the North East's new Regional Music Centre at Gateshead. Technical assistance has enabled the Orchestra to produce a complete four-year development plan which will expand its scale, its repertoire, its sphere of activities, and an audience to fill the new concert hall on its opening. With the Birmingham Rep, this is one of the most artistically inspired and radical strategies facilitated by the pilot programme. It will comprehensively raise the Orchestra's quality and profile over the next few years and help sustain artistically the Arts Council's heavy Lottery investment in new buildings for the arts in the region. The financial award will meet the exceptional short-term costs of new commissions, new activities and a sustained marketing and income development campaign.'
(Arts Council Press Release 19 Sep 1997)

In May 1999, formal submission was made to the Arts Council of England, with a document *Mission – Music*, marking an important step forward in The Sage Gateshead project (the new name bestowed in 2002 following a £6 million sponsorship deal with The Sage Group plc). After 10 years' planning and more than two-and-a-half years of detailed project development by the original partners, Northern Sinfonia, Folkworks, Northern Arts and Gateshead Council, the land at Gateshead Quays, owned by Gateshead Council, was at last committed to house what will surely prove one of the most iconographic buildings of the twenty-first century, the first Norman Foster building for the performing arts.

Architects Foster and Partners had been chosen via a RIBA competition, and set about producing detailed designs in consultation with the partners. There can be no doubt about the claim: 'They have produced an external form which is simultaneously unique, beautiful, startling and immediately "at home" in its historic surroundings...' and the site itself, one of unique prominence on the south side of the Tyne, opposite the fine architecture of Newcastle proper, has justly been called 'one of Europe's most dramatic urban sites.'

From inside looking out, the experience is equally impressive: '(the) foyers and public spaces will be open 16 hours a day and will provide spectacular view of the Tyne, its bridges and Newcastle.' (*Friends News* Dec 1998) The capital cost of the building was covered by the largest Arts Council Lottery grant ever given outside London, along with contributions from the Regional Development Agency, One NorthEast, European funds and Gateshead Council – the grant being confirmed in November 1999.

To sustain and underpin the international artistic programme (including but not exclusively that of the Orchestra in both performance and education) to be created in and from The Sage Gateshead, the project's management built the first major endowment fund for the arts in the UK; founding patrons include The Sage Group plc, The Barbour Trust, Northern Rock Foundation, The Garfield Weston Foundation and Joan and Margaret Halbert.

The progress of the building is neatly catalogued in the *Friends Newsletters*. In December 1998 came the news that 'A short while ago the design of the new Music Centre to be built at Gateshead was unveiled.' By March 2000 preparation of the site was underway, with reclamation of the site by Hall Construction Services of Rushyford, 'The next thing you will see as building work progresses is the completion of the retaining wall which will rise behind *HMS Calliope* and define the bank up from South Shore Road to the foot of the new building.' In mid-2001, building work was commenced by Laing: '... The Music Centre itself is now starting to appear out of the ground. The three yellow tower cranes next to the Tyne Bridge mark the site.' By September of the same year, it was reported, 'The piling is now complete and you can see the form of the three halls starting to take shape.' Throughout 2002 and 2003 the structure rose to its full height, the curvaceous lines of the roof began to be visible, and external girdering was covered, panel by panel, by the glass and stainless steel panels that form its dazzling outer skin.

The short trip across the Tyne (since plans were begun with the Marlborough Crescent Bus Station in mind) seems like nothing in comparison to the long journey Northern Sinfonia has made from its tentative start in 1958. Yet both have been remarkable achievements – and promise a wonderful new collaboration that will place the North East at the centre of the national musical consciousness: 'a landmark building on an exceptional site at the heart of the Region but operating regionally, nationally and internationally.' (*Mission – Music*)

Many have shared the feelings of the General Director of The Sage Gateshead, Anthony Sargent,

> '... as our new home reaches the exciting moment when its final shape is fully visible for the first time.

*The Sage Gateshead under construction (2004)*

In spring 2003 we marked the symbolic moment when our building reached its highest point; the proudly arching roofline at the east end, over the larger of our two main performance halls...'
(*NS Music* May–Jul 2003)

With the 17 December 2004 fixed as the date for the opening of the completed building, Anthony Sargent reflected:

'Finally, in 2004, Tyneside will finally play its full role on the international music stage when The Sage Gateshead opens its doors to the public. Northern Sinfonia has been at the heart of the project throughout its development, and it is absolutely fitting that it takes a unique role in its new home – not only as the backbone for all the classical programming in The Sage Gateshead with its own programme under Music Director, Thomas Zehetmair, but also in welcoming other internationally acclaimed musicians to its new home, and acting worldwide as a proud ambassador for Tyneside. The last year has seen the Orchestra triumphantly back at the Edinburgh, Bath and Aldeburgh Festivals and the BBC Proms, and playing some of the greatest halls in the world including The Philharmonie in Berlin, The Musikverein in Vienna and Amsterdam's Concertgebouw. Now all that is crowned by Northern Sinfonia taking the unique step of becoming a central part of the management of its own spectacular Norman Foster home.' (Sep 2004)

The start of another chapter.

*The Sage Gateshead (2004). Image courtesy of Simon Veit-Wilson.*

## Thanks

'Many individuals, trusts and foundations and companies have given very generously over the lifetime of the Orchestra. The backbone of the 1992–94 Appeal were those who were credited at the time as Founding Benefactors. In addition, we are greatly indebted to those individuals who supported the Orchestra through the Cornerstone Appeal in the late '90s. Many of these supporters continue to support Northern Sinfonia today through the Principal Partners scheme or other personal donations, memberships and purchases. We would like to take this opportunity to warmly thank all those who have supported the Orchestra in the past, and those who do so today. We also want to place on permanent record our huge appreciation for the constant support and commitment of the Arts Council, locally and nationally, throughout the history of the Orchestra.'

The Sage Gateshead, 2004

# APPENDICES

## 1. Officers of the Orchestra

Chairmen of the Northern Sinfonia Concert Society Ltd (North Music Trust from 2001)

Sir Humphrey Noble, Bart, MBE 1961–68
Charles Brackenbury 1968–1969
Anthony Jelly 1969–1972
Hans Lesser 1972–1975
William R. S. Forsyth 1975–1981
Cyril J Davies 1981–1988
Nigel Sherlock 1988–1990
Tony Pender 1990–1999
Stella Robson 1999–2001

## Artistic Directors / Conductors of Northern Sinfonia

Michael Hall 1958–1964
Rudolf Schwarz (Artistic Director and Principal Conductor) 1964–1973
Boris Brott (Joint Principal Conductor) 1964–1967
Christopher Seaman (Artistic Director and Principal Conductor) 1973–1979
Tamás Vásáry and Iván Fischer (Music Directors) 1979–1982
Richard Hickox (Artistic Director) 1982–1990
Heinrich Schiff (Artistic Director) 1990–1996
Jean-Bernard Pommier (Artistic Director) 1996–1999
Thomas Zehetmair (Music Director) 2002– present day

## General Managers

Antony Cullen 1960–1961
Colin Ratcliffe 1961–1966
Keith Statham 1966–1974
Christopher Yates 1974–1980
Martin Manasse 1980–1989
John Summers (Chief Executive) 1989–1999
Andrew Bennett (Chief Executive) 1999–2001
Simon Clugston (Performance Programme Director) 2001– present day

## 2. Members of Northern Sinfonia

This list attempts to bring together all the contracted ('permanent') players as at end 2004. There were, by definition, no contracted players prior to 1961, and some early concert programmes do not include an orchestral list. Coverage of this period is therefore, with regret, omitted, though we can trace the Leaders of the Orchestra at this time: Leonard Friedman 1958–1959, Kenneth Sillito 1959–1960, and Marie Wilson 1960–1961.

### Leaders

Michael Jones 1961–1964

Joseph Segal Acting Leader 1964–1965, Leader 1965–1969

Christopher Hirons 1969–1970, Co–Leader 1970–1973

Jack Rothstein 1970–1971

Barry Wilde 1971–1982

Bradley Creswick 1984–1987

Paul Barritt 1988–1994

Lesley Hatfield Co–Leader 1990–1995

Bradley Creswick 1994–present day

Kyra Humphreys Co–Leader 1997– present day

### Violins

Graham Bain
Paul Barritt
Robin Benefield
William Benham
Ronald Birks
Santiago Bravo
Noel Broome
Iona Brown
Marie Brown
Simon Browne
Shelagh Burns
Colin Callow
Peter Campbell-Kelly
Harry Cawood
Jenny Chang
Bradley Creswick
Teresa Cullis
Edwin Dodd
Susan Eaton
Nicholas Fallowfield
Carolyn Franks
Joanne Green
Tristan Gurney
Gillian Habgood
Lesley Hatfield
Marion Hillier
Christopher Hirons
Helen Hossack
Carole Howat
Martin Hughes
Katie Hull
Kyra Humphreys
Lucy Jeal
Michael Jones
Rosamund Kitchen
Clive Lander
Ann Lawes
Kay Lomax
Annamaria McCool
Peter Markham
Sidney Mann
Crawford Massey
Rolette de Montet
Julie Monument
Jane Pamment
Richard Panting
Elizabeth Payne
Peter Pople
Joanne Quigley
Linda Rhodes
Bransby Roberts
Sarah Roberts
Nicholas Rolfe
Gillian Rosefield
David Roth
Jack Rothstein
Joseph Segal
Helen Silverman
Jonathan Storer
Michael Stowe
Sylvia Sutton
Naomi Thomas
Geoffrey Ulman
Barry Wilde

**Violas**
Roger Best
Martin Bloor
Catherine Bradshaw
Frederick Crawshaw
Malcolm Critten
Antony Cullen
Michael Gerrard
Tegwen Jones
Susanne Martens
Prunella Pacey
Robert Smissen
Colin Start
Heather Wallington
Andrew Williams

**Cellos**
Susanne Beer
Ruth Bennett
Rosie Biss
James Craig
Christopher Gough
Maureen Lovell
Jeanette Mountain
Emma-Jane Murphy
Adam Skeaping
Alexander Somov
Deborah Thorne
Alan Turner
Tom Waddington

**Double-bass**
Roberto Carrillo-Garcia
Gail Jensen
Bryan Maynard
Jane McDermott
David Munro

**Flute**
David Haslam
Eva Stewart

**Oboe**
Marios Argiros
Sarah Barrington
Anthony Camden
Gareth Hulse
Colin Kellett
Helen Powell
Geoffrey Wareham
John Williams
Roger Winfield

**Clarinet**
Robert Ault
Graham Evans
Dov Goldberg
George MacDonald
Robert Plane
Chris Richards
Michael Whight

**Bassoon**
Meyrick Alexander
Michael Chapman
Stephen Reay
Ronald Thorndycraft
Geoffrey Walker

**Trumpet**
Clarence Adoo
Richard Martin
Marion Wilson

**French Horn**
Clare Briggs
Peter Francomb
Christopher Griffiths
Norman Horrod
Jan Keay
Hugh Potts
John Rooke
Bryan Sampson
Martin Shillito

**Percussion**
Alan Fearon
Layton Ring

# Bibliography and Sources

Cover image and drawing of All Saints Church, Quayside, and sketch of violinist by W. Holmes.

**Reference is made to:**

AGM – reports at Annual General Meetings of Northern Sinfonia (Archive 1/1)

Finance Mins – Finance Sub-committee Minutes (Archive 1/4)

Man. Mins – Management Committee Minutes (Archive 1/2)

Newspaper cuttings and magazine articles preserved in scrapbooks covering 1957–1987 (Archive 5/1)

Notes and tapes of interviews and correspondence 2003–2004 (Archive 7).

**Sources:**

Tony Froud, Concerts Manager Jul 1967–Mar 1989

Val Jobe, Current Chair of the Ladies Committee

Valentine Orde, OBE

Tom Little, the music critic from *The Northern Echo*

Tom Bergman, the *Evening Chronicle*

Arthur Milner, *The Journal*

John Healy, *The Journal*

Alistair Cox – Headmaster of Royal Grammar School.

**Publications:**

*25: Northern Sinfonia of England Silver Jubilee Year Prospectus 1983/84* edited by Tony Froud.

*40 Years of Northern Sinfonia: reflecting on the past and looking to the future* (1988).

*Friends News* – the Newsletters of Friends of Northern Sinfonia, edited by Jim Craigie.

*Music* – The Sage Gateshead magazine.

*Yearbook 1992 – The Inside Story*, edited by Stephen Cashman.

And to the various prospectuses/yearbooks, programmes and brochures issued by the Northern Sinfonia.

**Newspapers and Magazines:**

*BBC Music*
*Classical Music*
*Cleveland Evening Gazette*
*Evening Chronicle*
*Hannoversche Presse*
*Kölnische Rundschau*
*Main-Echo*
*Middlesbrough Evening Gazette*
*Music Teacher*
*New Society*
*Northern Despatch*
*Records & Recordings*
*Stage and TV Today*
*Stuttgarter Nachrichten*
*The Durham County Advertiser*
*The Guardian*
*The Journal*
*The Northern Echo*
*The Times*
*The Viewer*
*Volksblatt*

**Radio:**

*Third Programme – BBC*

**Television Programmes:**

*A Chamber Orchestra in Newcastle? You must be mad – BBC*
*Behind the bow-ties – Tyne Tees*
*The Magic of Music – Tyne Tees*
*The Making of Music – Tyne Tees*
*The Meisel Mystery – Tyne Tees*
*Your Kind of Music – Tyne Tees*
*Workshop BBC*